Delivering on the Promise

THE EDUCATION REVOLUTION

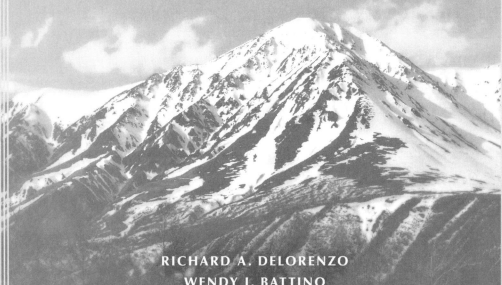

RICHARD A. DELORENZO

WENDY J. BATTINO

RICK M. SCHREIBER

BARBARA GADDY CARRIO

Solution Tree | Press

a division of
Solution Tree

555 North Morton Street
Bloomington, IN 47404
800.733.6786 (toll free) / 812.336.7700
FAX: 812.336.7790

email: info@solution-tree.com
solution-tree.com

Printed in the United States of America

12 11   3 4 5

FSC
Mixed Sources
Product group from well-managed
forests and other controlled sources

Cert no. SW-COC-002283
www.fsc.org
© 1996 Forest Stewardship Council

ISBN 978-1-934009-42-0

This book is dedicated to students . . . our future.

Acknowledgments

We extend our heartfelt gratitude and respect to the Alaskan villages of Chenega Bay, Icy Bay, Tatitlek, Two Moon Bay, and Whittier for their courage to do the right thing for their children and to lead the way toward an education system that works for every child.

We recognize the dedicated staff of the Chugach School District for putting themselves on the line and inspiring others.

We recognize Adams 50 School District, Denver, Colorado, as the largest and first district outside the state of Alaska to seriously commit to reinventing its system.

We offer a special thank you to Kirsten Miller for her always-first-rate writing and editorial support.

We are grateful to the Re-Inventing Schools Coalition staff and board for their continuing support and commitment to transforming education in the United States.

Finally, we recognize the schools and districts that are members of the Re-Inventing Schools Coalition. In particular, our deepest appreciation goes to Steve Atwater, Greg Johnson, Rebecca Midles, and Mark Standley for offering their experience, ideas, support, and time, over and over again during the writing of this book.

Table of Contents

About the Authors

Richard A. DeLorenzo is cofounder and consultant for the Re-Inventing Schools Coalition (RISC) and an internationally known leader in education and organization restructuring.

DeLorenzo is best known for his uniquely comprehensive grassroots approach to reinventing school systems. DeLorenzo led the first K–12 district in the United States, Alaska's Chugach School District, as it moved from a time-based system to a performance-based system in which students must meet performance targets to graduate instead of earning credits. Under DeLorenzo's leadership as assistant superintendent and later superintendent, this historically challenged rural district made remarkable strides in student achievement and became one of the first-ever education recipients of the prestigious Malcolm Baldrige National Quality Award. He is the creative vision behind *A Guide to Reinventing Schools* (Schreiber & Battino, 2002).

DeLorenzo has more than 24 years of experience working with high-risk youth and students with disabilities of all ages in a wide variety of settings, from urban classrooms of 30 multiage elementary students to rural school settings of at-risk secondary pupils.

Often described as a visionary, DeLorenzo has the unique ability to involve others in his dreams for advancing the education system—specifically, making changes thought to be impossible a reality. In addition to guiding schools and districts in the United States, DeLorenzo has consulted with organizations around the globe.

DeLorenzo earned a B.A. in Education, Special Education, from Central Washington University. He received an M.E., Special Education, and an educational administration degree from the University of Alaska, Juneau. He earned his superintendent credentials from the University of Alaska, Anchorage. DeLorenzo can be contacted at 80 Gold Creek Loop, Carlton, WA 98814. Phone: 509.923.2484. Email: rdelorenzo@gci.net

Wendy J. Battino is a cofounder and executive director of the Re-Inventing Schools Coalition (RISC).

Battino began her formal education career working with students who did not fit in the traditional system. She soon realized that a focus on innovations was imperative to meeting the needs of all students. Through this recognition, she began a journey to improve school systems across all boundaries. Experience at the classroom, school, and district levels provided Battino with an extensive background in standards-based instruction and assessment, school improvement planning, and curriculum design.

Battino seeks to solve educational problems through collaboration and research. As a testament to this commitment, she was integral in the initial development of the RISC Approach to Schooling through her grassroots efforts in teambuilding and continuous improvement.

Battino is the author of one of the first award-winning applications in education for the Malcolm Baldrige National Quality Award for the Chugach School District. She has worked with numerous organizations, in the U.S. and abroad, that are committed to transforming their education systems based on the RISC Approach to Schooling. For a number of years, Battino also was an education consultant with the Alaska Staff Development Network.

Battino was a principal teacher with the Chugach School District during the time that the district reinvented its education system. During her time with the district, she was one of the key individuals who designed and implemented the district's K–12 performance-based system. She also developed and implemented thematic units, assessments, and instructional approaches across all content areas, facilitated the Anchorage House Program, the district's school-to-life program, and coauthored *A Guide to Reinventing Schools* (Schreiber & Battino, 2002).

Battino demonstrates her belief in community involvement by volunteering at a local public radio station where she reports the news on Monday nights. She also is an elected board member of the Talkeetna Community Council, an Emergency Medical Technician, and Swift Water Responder. Her passion for creating extends to log building as well. She often conducts work from the log cabin she built with her husband, Rick Schreiber, in Talkeetna, Alaska.

Battino earned her B.A. in English from the University of California, Berkeley, and a secondary English endorsement from the University of Alaska. She can be contacted at P.O. Box 396, Talkeetna, Alaska 99676. Phone: 907.733.7400. Email: wbattino@reinventingschools.org

Rick M. Schreiber is cofounder and director of operations for the Re-Inventing Schools Coalition (RISC).

Schreiber has spent many years guiding and facilitating systemic school reform as a head teacher, staff and curriculum developer, consultant, and executive. Schreiber has a passion for helping schools and districts build cohesion through systematic processes to accomplishing common goals, and is well versed in using standards-based approaches to carry out these goals. Schreiber has consulted with schools and districts, both in the United States and abroad, that are committed to transforming their approach to education.

Schreiber has extensive experience in using evaluative methods related to school improvement efforts. He has been the team leader for onsite evaluations of RISC implementation efforts since 2004.

Schreiber cowrote the Chugach School District's award-winning application for the Malcolm Baldrige National Quality Award. Schreiber was a head teacher with the district during the time that the district reinvented its education system. He also is a coauthor of *A Guide to Reinventing Schools* (Schreiber & Battino, 2002).

Schreiber earned a B.A. in cultural ecology from Humboldt State University and a K–8 teaching certificate from the University of Alaska, Southeast. He can be contacted at P.O. Box 396, Talkeetna, Alaska 99676. Phone: 907.733.7400. Email: rschreiber@reinventingschools.org

Barbara Gaddy Carrio is a writer with extensive experience in the field of education, specifically standards-based approaches to schooling.

Gaddy Carrio was director of development communications at the University of Denver. She subsequently joined the staff of Mid-continent

Research for Education and Learning (McREL), where she worked closely with Robert Marzano and then was managing editor of publications under McREL's regional educational laboratory contract with the U.S. Department of Education. She later served as chief executive officer and project manager for Marzano & Associates, Inc.

Gaddy Carrio's publication credits include *A Handbook for Classroom Management that Works* (Marzano, Gaddy, Foseid, Foseid, & Marzano, 2005), *Classroom Management That Works: Facilitator's Guide* (Marzano, Gaddy, & D'Arcangelo, 2004), *A Handbook for Classroom Instruction that Works* (Marzano, Norford, Paynter, Pickering, & Gaddy, 2001), *Essential Knowledge: The Debate Over What American Students Should Know* (Marzano & Kendall, with Gaddy, 1999), and *School Wars: Resolving Our Conflicts Over Religion and Values* (Gaddy, Hall, & Marzano, 1996).

Gaddy Carrio earned a B.S. in Marketing Management from Miami University in Oxford, Ohio, and an M.A. in Mass Communications from the University of Denver. She can be contacted at 5401 S. Park Terrace Avenue, A-205, Greenwood Village, CO 80111. Phone: 303.378.8586. Email: bgaddycarrio@comcast.net

Preface

North America is filled with smart and engaging teachers who use effective teaching strategies in their classrooms, develop positive relationships with their students, find ways to make content meaningful, individualize instruction, and motivate students to do their best—including those students others think are not capable or motivated to learn.

Most of us were lucky enough to have at least one of these great teachers, whom we may remember to this day. One of mine was Mr. Keigley, my fifth-grade teacher in Arlington Heights, Illinois. I remember all the ways in which he encouraged me and pointed out my strengths. He probably never knew it, but he inspired me to be a writer.

It is primarily a matter of luck whether a student has a teacher like Mr. Keigley. The philosophy of education highlighted in this book—the Re-Inventing Schools Coalition (RISC) Approach to Schooling—aims to create systems that do not leave it to chance. *Every* student should have access to great teachers, not just the few students lucky enough to be in their classes. Every child should have access to great teaching—in every content area, in every year of his or her K–16 experience.

Like all parents, I also wanted this for my son, Brian. In middle school, Brian was fortunate to have an excellent educational experience. But for much of the rest of his elementary and secondary education, school was frustrating, unrewarding, and not academically challenging, in spite of attending two of the best schools in the Denver Public Schools system and having good teachers for most of those years.

In second and third grade, for instance, Brian spent a great deal of time essentially teaching other students. Meanwhile, he was not challenged himself and felt more and more different and separate, as if something was wrong with him. For example, one day his second-grade teacher asked him to pick a challenging book in the classroom to read. When he did not pick one, she confronted him as though he had done something wrong.

"Why didn't you pick a book to read?" she asked.

"Because there is no book in here that's challenging to me," he answered.

By fourth grade, it was clear that Brian needed a different academic experience. At the urging of his principal, a teacher, and my good friend and colleague Bob Marzano, and after some testing, we enrolled Brian in a school for gifted children. He spent 4 years there, which ended up being the best part of his K–16 educational experience. He quickly grew to love learning and was engaged and challenged academically to move well beyond the content typically specified for 10- to 13-year-olds.

In high school, Brian entered the International Baccalaureate (IB) program, widely viewed as one of the best high school educational programs in the world. During his freshman year, motivated by the challenge of doing well in the highly touted IB program, he earned nearly straight As. But by the end of that first high school year, his motivation to do his best had fallen away. He became disengaged, uninterested, and irritated at the highly structured program; his grades slipped, and he began to do everything he could to simply get by and get out. With less than 5 months to go before graduating with an IB diploma, he dropped out of the program, signed up for a couple of Advanced Placement classes, and graduated from high school early.

Brian subsequently attended a large public university in Colorado and graduated with a double major. Today he is productive, working, and seems satisfied to some extent, but I have the sense that his work life is not the fullest expression of his passion, intellect, and desire to make a difference in the world. He is considering what is next for his future: whether to throw himself fully into his current work field, go to graduate school or law school, or pursue something else he loves.

My son is making a good life for himself, to be sure. His insight, drive, and intelligence will take him far. But I see the impact of those years of schooling that were so frustrating and disengaging. Most of all, I see the missed opportunity of his K–16 years.

What was the problem with my son's education? After all, he had a number of very good teachers here and there.

The missing ingredient was a *system* of schooling across his K–16 years, a system that continually created an environment in which he flourished to the fullest extent of his abilities with his unique perspectives of himself and the world; one that tapped into, crystallized, and helped him realize his vision for life; one that allowed and encouraged him to move through his studies at his own pace and inspired him to be and do his best—a system with the flexibility to meet his educational needs while meeting the varied needs of his fellow students.

Many schools claim to be doing this, with all the best intentions, but there is no systematic approach to ensure that it happens—and that it happens at every level of schooling. Conversely, in schools and districts implementing the RISC Approach to Schooling, this is done intentionally and measured and improved over time. I often wonder what might have been possible if my son had been in that kind of school system throughout *all* the years of his educational career.

For a significant part of my work life, I have worked in the field of education in various capacities. I enjoyed my past jobs and am grateful for the many opportunities I have had, but I have often questioned whether education is really my "thing."

A large part of my past work entailed editing and writing reports and briefs. After a while, it occurred to me that there were about 100 words used over and over, in report after report, but in different ways, as if there were a big jumbler that moved the words around. That is not surprising in one sense; after all, any field or specialty has terms and phrases that convey a shared understanding. But there were times when I could not see how those words made a deep and lasting difference in real students' lives. Frequently, they were words on a page, rather than expressions of vital concepts alive in our education system.

Over the course of working with the leaders of the Re-Inventing Schools Coalition and learning more about its philosophy of education and the many students it has aided, I have often thought of those words we used over and over. They finally have real meaning. Perhaps if I had known about this system of education and had the opportunity to work closely with this team of educators years ago, education would have been my "thing" all along.

—Barbara Gaddy Carrio
Greenwood Village, Colorado

From a Time-Based to a Performance-Based System: A Necessary Transformation

Leading Questions

1. What are the attitudes in your school or district about teaching and learning? Do you believe that *all* children can learn?

2. Do your school or district standards include 21st-century standards that span content areas such as critical thinking, creativity, innovation, teamwork, and leadership?

3. Do you think that the assessments required by your state result in an accurate picture of student learning?

4. What is the situation in your community in terms of graduation rates, dropouts, applications for postsecondary education, and graduates' readiness to compete in the global workforce?

5. As a teacher or administrator, are you willing to make substantive changes in your practices if you see the potential benefits?

6. What would it take to revolutionize the education system to create a virtual 24/7 system?

Many people cannot wait for the day when the use of auto fuel cells is as normal as talking on a cell phone to a friend or searching the Internet on a Blackberry. On that day, you will no longer need to stop at the local Fill-Er-Up Gas Station, stand in the cold, rain, sleet, or blazing heat while you fumble around for your credit card, figure out the instructions on the screen you can never read, eventually fill up your gas tank, and then drive away, invariably with the smell of gasoline on your hands.

Picture, instead, driving up to a Fuel Cell Renewal Station, where a smiling attendant zips out to greet you, pops open the hood of your car, replaces your old fuel cell with a brand new one, electronically sends you a bill in a flash, then pats your car on the rear bumper and cheerily says, "See you next year!"

When this happy day arrives, a number of things about our current vehicles will be obsolete: the gas tank, the fuel intake opening, the fuel line, and so on. Auto designers and engineers looking ahead to that day are probably not thinking about how to replace the gas line with a fuel cell. Rather, they are likely creating a completely new design for the entire system of the automobile, not just its fuel-related components. These dramatic changes will naturally affect the automotive and gas industries, but will have other ramifications influencing economic sectors well beyond these industries.

A similar moment is before us in education. For years we have been trying to change, adjust, and tweak the existing traditional education system, when what we need is a fundamentally different system. In other words, to use the fuel cell analogy, we have largely focused our attention and resources on adjusting the size of the gas tank, rearranging how the fuel line relates to the engine, and otherwise trying to improve the efficiency of the gasoline system, instead of challenging the "givens." In the traditional education system, the most notable givens are seat-time-based graduation requirements and A–F grading, which most of us have regarded as untouchable. Until we are willing to challenge these givens, we are likely to see some overall improvements in student achievement, but not the kind of significant, sustainable increases that are possible—for all students—when an education system encourages and is organized around the individual ways in which human beings learn and grow.

The Traditional Time-Based, Credit-Driven System

The traditional education system is familiar to all of us. Students are grouped into age-based grade levels and progress through the years, grade level to grade level, by completing a certain amount of seat time each year and earning a minimum grade, typically a D–, in required courses, in order to earn the 22 or so Carnegie unit credits required for graduation. Students at each grade level are taught the same content in a particular school or district. All first graders, typically 6- and 7-year-olds, are taught the same set of knowledge and skills; all second graders, typically 7- and 8-year-olds, are taught the same set of knowledge and skills; and so on. A few students skip ahead a grade level, but when they do, they move ahead in all content areas. Until sometime in middle school, students who do not earn a minimum grade are held back and must repeat all of the content and courses for that grade level.

In the traditional education system, school boards and administrators determine the courses that students must complete successfully in order to graduate. In addition, the specific content that is taught in one class frequently is quite different from that taught by another teacher of the same grade level and content area.

In this system, although grades are viewed as all-important (whose parent did not applaud the A and frown on the D?), what matters more are credits. In fact, an A in a required course earns the same number of credits for graduation as a D–. The A student and the D– student each are granted a high school diploma, yet the D– student graduates with less than a 1.0 GPA, essentially illiterate and uneducated.

In some states, credits are no longer enough, but the new bar may not be much higher. As of the 2007–2008 school year, students in 23 states—representing 68% of all public high school students and 75% of all minority public high school students—must pass a high school exit exam to receive a diploma, even if they have earned all of the credits required for graduation (Center on Education Policy [CEP], 2008). However, in most of the 23 states where these controversial tests are required, the exams are aligned with 10th-grade content standards. In a few states, grade-level alignment is as low as eighth grade. Indeed, California's math test aligns with the state's Algebra I standards, designed to be taught across grades 8–12, but also with the state's math standards for grades 6–7 (CEP, 2008).

State-mandated high school exit exams are in place for a variety of reasons: to ensure that graduates have a certain level of competency in required content areas, to provide data to state policymakers about the extent to which students have reached state education goals, to meet the assessment requirements of the No Child Left Behind Act, and to prepare students for the world of work beyond high school. However, questions about the unintended, negative consequences of these exams—in terms of numbers of high school dropouts, impacts on students with disabilities and students of color, whether students have had sufficient opportunities to learn assessed content, and other concerns—have led to lawsuits, most notably in Arizona and California. Despite legal challenges to high school exit exams, the number of states that will mandate them is expected to grow to 26 by 2012 (CEP, 2008).

Over the past several years, a number of states have begun to move toward requiring high school end-of-course exams designed to better assess students' mastery of the content of a specific course. In several states, these exams will replace required high school exit exams; in three other states, end-of-course exams will be administered along with required high school exit exams. Some of the states that do not use (or plan to use) an exit exam as a criterion for graduation still use testing in one form or another to motivate students. For example, in hopes of encouraging postsecondary attendance, six states—Colorado, Illinois, Kentucky, Maine, Michigan, and Wyoming—require all students to take the SAT or ACT college entrance exams (CEP, 2008).

Whether the intent behind them is punitive or inspirational, wherever these or similar policies have been implemented, questions regarding equity and opportunity to learn have followed in their wake: Have students been given adequate opportunities to learn the content covered by these exams, particularly those with high stakes?

Questions arise, in part, because the traditional education system is primarily a passive learning environment. The energy and momentum of schooling moves from teachers to students. As a whole, students take little ownership of the educational process, wait for their teachers to tell them what to do, and view their courses as something to survive in order to move ahead.

Struggling students get assistance, but many are passed along to the next grade level with little academic knowledge and low-level skills. Some advanced and gifted students excel, but many others are bored and become disengaged while waiting for other students to catch up. Many good teachers try to adjust their instruction to reach all of their students, but established structures and policies, as well as the culture itself, make individualized approaches difficult to implement successfully over time. In addition, administrators and teachers are often mired in complying with policies and mandates, a condition that leaves little room for innovation and creativity.

Education Reform

Since the 1960s, numerous reports and studies from the business, non-profit, and education sectors have been published relating to the condition of American public education, its strengths and weaknesses (primarily its weaknesses), and national and international trends in education and global competitiveness. The extent of the criticism has been substantial; and the results of these studies, beginning with the well-known Coleman report (1966) ordered by President Lyndon Johnson, have significantly and negatively affected public views of educational opportunity in the United States.

In the early 1980s through the early 1990s, other publications raised our collective blood pressure by describing the rapidly expanding and ever-more-interconnected global and technogically driven economy, in which U.S. students were unprepared to compete successfully. *A Nation at Risk: The Imperative for Educational Reform,* published in 1983 by the National Commission on Excellence in Education, took alarm to a new level. The report sent a distress signal with its opening paragraph:

> Our Nation is at risk. Our once unchallenged preeminence in commerce, industry, science, and technological innovation is being overtaken by competitors throughout the world. . . . What was unimaginable a generation ago has begun to occur—others are matching and surpassing our educational attainments. (para. 1)

The Standards Movement

A Nation at Risk had a dramatic, long-lasting effect on U.S. public education. In many ways, it was the final word on the failure of U.S. public schools. However, this highly influential report led to at least one significant, positive, and lasting outgrowth: the beginning of the standards movement.

From the mid-1980s through the 1990s, states set academic standards in many content areas. (For an excellent overview of the history of the standards movement, see Kendall & Marzano, 2004.) By 2002, 49 states (all except Iowa) had established state-level academic standards.

These standards provided a critical missing piece of the public education system: statements articulating what students should know and be able to do at various stages of their K–12 education and before graduating from high school. In tandem with this benefit, the standards movement also established that Americans wanted students to attain a higher academic bar than in the past; in other words, students should demonstrate a deep level of understanding and a high degree of skill in the content required at each grade level.

Today, standards are an integral element of schooling in the United States at the local, state, and national levels. The extent to which schools and districts are truly aligning their systems around standards varies tremendously, and there are great weaknesses in understanding and implementation, yet today standards are a core concept in any conversation about American education.

The No Child Left Behind Act

One very public outgrowth of the standards movement has been the No Child Left Behind Act (NCLB), developed with bipartisan support and signed into law by President George W. Bush in January 2002. Among other provisions, the law mandates that 100% of students in every state be proficient in reading and mathematics on state exams no later than the end of the 2013–2014 school year, and that all subgroups of students in every school and district make adequate yearly progress (AYP) toward realizing this goal.

Passing NCLB was like shining a surgical lamp on our failure to effectively educate all students, making ever more clear the fact that we have indeed left more than one child behind. One of the positive outcomes of

NCLB is that for the first time, we as a nation are looking systematically at our schools, scrutinizing student achievement data, and evaluating how we do business in education. Whereas the catchphrase of the standards movement might be "academic standards—set 'em high," NCLB's most certainly is "accountability, accountability, accountability."

There is significant debate about the law, its positive and negative consequences, whether student achievement has declined or improved as a result, whether the achievement gap has narrowed, and how specific aspects of the law should be interpreted. Nonetheless, it is a widely shared view among those on all sides of the issue that thousands of schools are not on track to ensure that all students are proficient in reading and math by 2014; these schools are failing, or will be failing, under NCLB requirements. No Child Left Behind has led to additional accountability, but its goal to bring 100% of students to proficiency in core subject areas in a few short years seems unlikely to be realized in the current education system.

Educating Students for the 21st Century

Successfully educating all students is a highly personal issue for every parent, whether we view our children as failing, lagging, average, advanced, or gifted. It also is a highly national issue.

It is not a novel statement to say that the world is increasingly an interdependent, global, technologically driven economy. Most of us have had firsthand experience of this; call your favorite accounting or banking software helpline for advice, for instance, and you are likely to be connected to a technical advisor stationed in India.

In addition to the 1983 publication of *A Nation at Risk*, two reports from the early 1990s further elevated our concern about the challenges of the changing world economy: *What Work Requires of Schools: A SCANS Report for America 2000* (U.S. Department of Labor, Secretary's Commission on Achieving Necessary Skills, 1991) and *America's Choice: High Skills or Low Wages! The Report of the Commission on the Skills of the American Workforce* (National Center on Education and the Economy, 1990). Together, these reports called on companies and educational institutions to transform themselves into high-performance organizations that would prepare and continually educate Americans to succeed in the dynamic, global workplace. Notably, the SCANS report identified the academic and thinking skills, personal qualities, and competencies that effective employees use seamlessly and simultaneously—and that are the mark of globally competitive companies in which distributed leadership, creativity, productivity, excellence, and quality define success in the workplace.

At the time of the publication of these reports, the impact of an increasingly global, digital economy was being more fully realized. The problem—and opportunity—that these reports pointed to is more true today than ever before, as more and more U.S. jobs are lost to overseas workers (both highly skilled and unskilled) who are willing to work for much lower wages (National Center on Education and the Economy, 2007).

For the most part, the U.S. education system ill-equips its students to succeed in this highly competitive, constantly changing environment. Although students leave high school armed with a stock of basic content knowledge, they largely lack the ability to apply that content knowledge in real-world settings. Today's students—tomorrow's employees—also need to learn and think on their feet, reason, creatively solve problems, and work in teams.

This skill set is just as applicable for the worker on the factory floor as it is for the management executive. Both must, for example, within the contexts of their individual jobs, be able to look ahead, anticipate challenges, and consider how their work is connected with that of their fellow employees across the system. The lack of competence in such skills can be more than an inconvenience; if a police officer and his partner are incapable of working as a team and seamlessly solving problems and making decisions, the consequences could be dire.

Furthermore, this skill set is just as critical for individuals to be effective citizens and community members as it is for them to be successful workers. Indeed, teamwork, problem solving, decision making, collaboration, and a host of other interpersonal skills are useful for any group of people, formally or informally assembled—as a neighborhood, city council, church group, or random strangers traveling together on the New York City subway. The value of these skills, and the role of our educational institutions in providing students with opportunities to develop them, is consistent with the view expressed by early U.S. political and education leaders and in a long line of public school court cases that schools are institutions where students are prepared to participate effectively as citizens in a democracy. See, in particular, U.S. Supreme Court cases Ambach v. Norwick (1979) and Brown v. Board of Education (1954), and *Democracy and Education: An Introduction to the Philosophy of Education* (Dewey, 1916).

The need for such applied skills—often referred to as *21st-century skills*—is garnering more attention. Appreciation for the value of these skills has led to the creation of groups such as the Partnership for 21st Century Skills, a "coalition of corporations and organizations that serves as a catalyst to position 21st century skills at the center of U.S. K–12 education by building collaborative partnerships among education, business, communities and government" (n.d., p. 2). As the Partnership has recognized, today's (and tomorrow's) market seeks employees who have a solid foundation of academic knowledge and skills, but who also have 21st-century skills—"the skills students need to succeed in work, school and life" (p. 1). In addition to core content knowledge, this skill set includes the following:

- **21st-century content**—global awareness, financial, economic, business and entrepreneurial literacy, civic literacy, and health and wellness awareness

- **Learning and thinking skills**—critical thinking and problem-solving skills, communications skills, creativity and innovation skills, collaboration skills, contextual learning skills, and information and media literacy skills

- **Information and communications technology literacy**

- **Life skills**—leadership, ethics, accountability, adaptability, personal productivity, personal responsibility, people skills, self-direction, and social responsibility (Partnership for 21st Century Skills, n.d., p. 1)

In addition to having a solid foundation in these skills, employees need to be *resilient* (able to adapt readily to changing job requirements and conditions), and able to learn the new knowledge and skills required to keep their current jobs and to find new ones (U.S. Department of Labor, 2006, p. 24). Graduating students will choose careers based on information available to them now, but consider the extent to which many career fields—medicine, engineering, computer technology, manufacturing, and communications, to name a few—are likely to change over the course of 5 years, let alone the 30, 40, or more years of an average person's work life.

Further, a graduate's first career choice will likely not be his or her last. The latest findings from a longitudinal survey being conducted by the U.S. Department of Labor's Bureau of Labor Statistics (2008) of nearly 10,000 working men and women born in the years 1957 to 1964 found that respondents had held an average of 10.8 jobs between the ages of 18 and 42. If this was true of today's students' *parents*, imagine what is true for the students themselves given the particularly fast-changing nature of today's global workplace.

The merging dynamics of global competitiveness and an increasingly technology-driven world point to the need to prepare students differently, in short, to prepare students to succeed in a world that does not yet exist. Although NCLB has raised the accountability bar, studies show that educators are largely focused on teaching the content covered on required state tests (CEP, 2006). For the most part, the larger, job-spanning skills discussed here are not being taught or assessed in U.S. public schools in a systematic way—but it has become increasingly clear that our children are not likely to succeed without them.

Student Achievement

Much can be said about the achievement of U.S. students—compared to each other and compared to their age peers in other countries—and whether student performance has increased or decreased, for which groups of students, and in which content areas. Under NCLB, individual states must ensure that all students are proficient in reading and mathematics by the end of the 2013–2014 school year; until then, they must make adequate yearly progress (AYP) toward that goal. How AYP is measured, however, is determined by states; specifically, each state sets its own standards for reading and mathematics and assigns benchmarks by which students will be judged "proficient." States are required to publicly report their progress toward AYP through annual state report cards.

Using state results as our barometer, we might think that students are doing quite well. Yet the results of a 2007 study conducted by the U.S. Department of Education (National Center for Education Statistics [NCES], 2007a) cast significant doubt on this conclusion. Using data from the 2004–2005 academic year, researchers mapped state proficiency standards in reading and mathematics onto the appropriate scale for the National Assessment of Educational Progress (NAEP), the only large-scale national assessment of U.S. students' knowledge and skill, and obtained NAEP score equivalents. Researchers used these score equivalents to compare the percentages of students who reached proficiency as defined by each state and the estimated percentage of students in each state who achieved proficiency as defined by NAEP.

The disparities between state and NAEP results are startling. In Mississippi, for example, 88% of fourth graders scored proficient or higher on the 2005 state reading assessment; yet only 18% scored at comparable levels on the NAEP—a gap of 70 percentage points. In contrast, in Massachusetts, the state with the highest number of college graduates, 48% of fourth graders scored proficient or higher on the state assessment, and 44% scored at the same level on the NAEP—a gap of just 4 percentage points (NCES, 2007b). Researchers concluded that "most of the heterogeneity across states in the NAEP score equivalents can be attributed to differences in the stringency of the proficiency standards set by the states" (NCES, 2007a, p. 2). At a minimum, these findings point to the great variance among states in how proficiency is defined; in other words, how high the academic bar is set varies widely across states. More realistically, however, these findings reveal the low standards set by many states for educating their students.

NAEP results themselves are instructive relative to the long-term performance of U.S. students. Dubbed "the nation's report card," the NAEP exam is given to a cross-section of students in all 50 states in grades 4, 8, and 12. The results from the 2004 NAEP in reading show statistically significant gains in achievement for 9-year-olds compared to the last assessment in

1999 and to 1971, the year of the first NAEP reading assessment. However, no such gains were found for 13-year-olds or for 17-year-olds. (See the NCES web site at http://nces.ed.gov/nationsreportcard for more information.) The gains achieved by 9-year-olds are good, to be sure, but on a scale from 0 to 500, the average reading scale score for 9-year-olds was 219 in 2004 compared to 212 in 1999 and 208 in 1971.

In terms of international comparisons, long-term assessment results are available from the Trends in International Mathematics and Science Study (TIMSS), formerly known as the Third International Mathematics and Science Study. TIMSS studies of students' mathematics and science achievement have been carried out since 1995 by the International Association for the Evaluation of Educational Achievement, an international organization of national research institutions and governmental research agencies (see NCES, n.d.).

Mathematics achievement data are available for students in fourth and eighth grade from the countries that participated in the 2003 TIMSS study (see NCES, http://nces.ed.gov/pubs2005/timss03). U.S. fourth-grade scores exceeded those in 13 of the 25 countries that participated in the math TIMSS, but American students were outperformed by their age peers in 11 countries—4 Asian countries (Singapore, Japan, Chinese Taipei, and Hong Kong SAR [Hong Kong is a Special Administrative Region (SAR) of the People's Republic of China]) and 7 European countries (Belgium-Flemish, England, Hungary, Latvia, Lithuania, Netherlands, and the Russian Federation). (See NCES, http://nces.ed.gov/pubs2005/timss03/xls/table_02.xls.) A number of those countries are important competitors in the global economy. In addition, TIMSS researchers found no measurable changes in the average scores of U.S. fourth graders in math (or science) between 1995 and 2003.

Relative to eighth grade, mathematics scores of U.S. students exceeded those of their peers in 30 of the 45 countries that participated in the 2003 TIMSS eighth-grade math assessment, but U.S. students were outperformed by their peers in 14 countries—a list that again includes a number of global competitors. TIMSS researchers found significant increases in U.S. eighth-grade math performance (and in the performance of students in a number of other countries) between 1995 and 2003, most of which occurred between 1995 and 1999.

Assessment results are one barometer of the degree to which schools are serving students; another is the high school graduation rate. Independent analyses of state graduation rates estimate that only 7 out of 10 students complete high school, and that the completion rate is much worse for students of color (Swanson, 2008). To put this in real terms, a projected 1.2 million students nationwide entered grade 9 in 2000–2001 but did not graduate in 2003–2004; more than half of these were African American, Latino, or Native American youth (Hall, 2005).

Dropout and graduation rates in the United States are a highly relevant topic. Comparisons between high school dropouts and those who graduate tell us much about the effectiveness of the U.S. education system as well as the potential future societal, workplace, and economic impacts of undereducated and unprepared young adults. For instance, dropouts are more likely to be unemployed, earn less, spend time in jail, rely on public assistance, and experience comparatively worse health than their high school graduate counterparts (Hall, 2005; Laird, Cataldi, KewalRamani, & Chapman, 2008).

Dropout rates and the assessment results discussed here are but a small sampling of the vast databank available relative to the performance of American students and the state of our schools. In short, viewed from one perspective, there are challenges with the U.S. education system; viewed from another perspective, we have a crisis on our hands. In terms of student achievement, we appear to have realized some gains. Nonetheless, no matter how we slice it, we are a long way from being able to make the claim that 100% of U.S. students have a proficient level of knowledge and skill in core subject areas, let alone that they are excelling and ready to successfully compete in U.S. and global marketplaces. We have tremendous ground to cover to attain the performance levels U.S. citizens desire for all of their students—to deliver on the promise of American education.

Challenging the Givens

To date, most efforts to improve the education system have failed because what was considered possible was limited by our shared, unquestioned assumptions and beliefs—our shared education paradigm. As Chris Whittle (2005) asserts in arguing for large-scale research and development in education, "Our schools remain stuck in the past" (p. 32).

One of the most basic assumptions of K–12 education is that of seat time and course credits. Measuring student progress by time and credits is such an ingrained part of American educational culture that it has largely remained unquestioned—even unacknowledged. Time and credits are to educators like water is to fish. They have been there so long that they are part of the culture, part of the background. This inability or unwillingness to consider changing something so fundamental is what Marzano, Zaffron, Zraik, Robbins, and Yoon (1995) call a "blind spot":

> One of the paradoxical features of paradigms is that their interpretative power creates unavoidable "blind spots" in our perceptions. That is, paradigms both enable and inhibit perception. On one hand, they provide frameworks with which to organize sensory stimuli; on the other hand, they limit what can be perceived because of inherent assumptions that underpin them. . . . [Paradigms] tell us what to do and what to expect in every situation without the need for deep philosophical consideration. (pp. 163–164)

The changes that most reform efforts have entailed have been only those possible within the existing paradigm of seat time and credits. As a result, education reform programs have not had the kind of dramatic, long-lasting effect on student achievement that is needed.

A Paradigm Shift—Transforming the Mission: Learning for All

Although paradigms are fixed, pervasive, and largely unseen, they do shift, a phenomenon introduced by Thomas Kuhn in his 1962 book *The Structure of Scientific Revolution* and since applied to many fields beyond science. As Marzano et al. (1995) discuss extensively, one of the ways in which paradigms shift is when a current worldview is considered to be "bankrupt." Stated differently, our shared view of reality about schooling will shift when we see that the current view no longer works.

The traditional education system was created some 150 years ago in a completely different economic and cultural time. The purpose of schooling at that point was to provide access to education for all students, a worthy and highly American goal. However, as influential University of Chicago President Robert Maynard Hutchins (1953, cited in Lezotte, 1997a, p. 3) is frequently quoted as saying:

> Perhaps the greatest idea that America has given the world is the idea of education for all. The world is entitled to know whether this idea means that everybody can be educated or simply that everybody must go to school.

These words are as significant today as they were when Hutchins first wrote them. For years, our approach to education was, "Every child must go to school; most will probably do okay." Now, our rhetoric has shifted to, "Every child must go to school, and every child *will meet* high standards."

But we have to ask ourselves whether our collective attention has been on all students learning, or on teaching and hoping to reach most students. Have we had a kind of bell-curve view of education, assuming that a certain percentage of students *will* fail, no matter what? Chris Whittle (2005) asserts that "as a nation we have come to accept that failure is an option, that it is 'just the way it is,' that it is somehow okay that tens of thousands of our schools don't work for the children within them" (p. 136). It is almost as though we have been whispering to each other, "I know we *say* all children can and will learn, but we don't really mean that, do we?"

It is imperative that many more of us—particularly superintendents, principals, policymakers, and others in key decision-making positions—commit to doing what it takes to ensure that all children learn. In other words, the order of business for public education, says Lezotte (1997), must be to "change the mission from compulsory schooling to compulsory learning" (p. 52).

Standards- and Performance-Based Education

Like all human beings, children learn and develop at different rates and in different ways; they learn different content at different rates and in different ways. Despite that, traditional education moves students through grade levels in age-similar groups. This approach may be less tumultuous socially than students working together across age levels, but it impacts students negatively in many other ways and is inconsistent with natural developmental differences that make people unique.

First, this process creates artificial constraints for students, constraints that are apparent in instruction and assessment. For example, eighth-grade state-level assessments must be taken by all eighth-grade students whether some are academically ready to take those assessments or not. Second, this approach stigmatizes "slow" students who fail tests, who take longer to learn specific content compared to other students, or who struggle with specific concepts and skills. These students are affected in other ways as well. For example, lagging students frequently are promoted to the next grade level after squeaking by with barely acceptable test or course grades. The gap in students' knowledge base that results from social promotion shows up in the next grade level, and the next and the next, and often is never remedied.

At the other end of the spectrum, gifted students may be just as out of sync with their age peers for other reasons. Even though gifted students generally are viewed as having an easy time of it in school, research and practice have repeatedly shown that many gifted students are exceptionally bright children with special needs, or *twice-exceptional* children (National Association for Gifted Children, 2005). A sixth-grade child, for example, may have college-level academic abilities *and* learning disabilities. Complicating the issue, being gifted can lead to anxiety, low self-esteem, and social diffi-culties for students as they struggle to fit in with their fellow students.

These brief examples illustrate the logic and importance of creating an education system that builds on and encourages, rather than impedes and stifles, the uniquely individual ways in which children learn and grow. The system that accomplishes these goals is one that allows students the freedom to move at their own pace—one that honors the natural develop-mental differences among students, yet holds them to high standards. Such a system—a truly standards- and performance-based system—reflects one of the most fundamental of American principles: the innate desire and drive to do and be our best as unique individuals.

The RISC Approach to Schooling: From a Time- to a Performance-Based System

As the National Center on Education and the Economy (2007) declared in *Tough Choices or Tough Times*, its report on the skills of the American workforce, "It is not possible to get where we have to go by patching that system. . . . We can get where we must go only by changing the system itself" (p. 8).

Together, the standards movement and its most influential policy outgrowth, the No Child Left Behind Act, have resulted in a new culture of accountability for all students meeting specific academic standards. The missing ingredient is a shift in our educational approach, from one in which students progress en masse by following uniform methods of earning credits or seat time and reaching relatively low levels of academic performance, to one in which students progress individually by demonstrating (in a variety of ways and at a self-defined pace) that they have reached high levels of academic performance. Our commitment to every child learning will only be realized through an integrated standards- and performance-based system that ensures every student reaches his or her potential—not just some students, or even most, or those with dedicated parents, or those in schools with tremendous financial resources.

What is needed is a system that can be replicated anywhere, by anyone, for any student, under any set of circumstances. This system represents a dramatic shift for America education, a literal reinvention of what schooling looks like.

The philosophy of education that is the focus of this book—the RISC Approach to Schooling—is about such a system, replicable and proven to work, that gives every child in America the best opportunity for success in life.

In the 1970s and early 1980s, in response to assertions that the U.S. education system was failing students, education researchers undertook numerous studies of the characteristics of effective schools. They developed a body of research that supported the idea that all children can learn, and that schools have within their control the factors needed to ensure that students master required content. (For a comprehensive synthesis of the effective schools research, see Marzano, 2000, and Good & Brophy, 1986.) The RISC Approach to Schooling (discussed in depth in chapter 3) draws on the broad body of guidance from leading educators who have synthesized these findings.

The RISC Approach to Schooling is a standards-based approach to education designed to educate all students to the highest levels, empower them to own and lead the learning process, help them realize their dreams, and equip them with the knowledge, skills, and abilities to succeed in a rapidly changing world. Motivation, engagement, and shared leadership—and clarity that *every* child can learn—are foundational pillars of RISC's whole-child model.

The RISC Approach to Schooling requires much more of students than the traditional approach to K–12 education—both in terms of students' academic peformance and their ownership of the learning process—but this approach makes much more possible for students as well. Very low-level, just-get-by achievement is no longer sufficient for advancement. Proficiency is the new bar for *every* student. There is a shared commitment to ensure that every student has a solid understanding, facility with skills, and the ability to interact effectively with real-world situations in every content area. In addition, students no longer simply wait for teachers to tell them what to do next. Instead, students, even very young ones, are empowered to partner with their teachers, lead, and participate in their own educational experience. At the same time, students are provided with the teaching, coaching, support, and individualized learning experiences they need to succeed.

The most fundamental difference between a traditional education system and a RISC system—one that translates into very practical differences—is that in a traditional system, time is the constant and learning is the variable. In a RISC system, the reverse is true: *Learning is the constant and time is the variable.*

As explained earlier, in a traditional system, students spend 13 years in school, kindergarten through grade 12, as they earn a certain amount of seat time each year by receiving a minimum grade, as low as a D–, in each required course. Whether they learn and to what extent they learn, however, varies greatly—from class to class, teacher to teacher, and school to school.

Conversely, in a school or district implementing the RISC approach, students move at their own pace (as fast or as slow as needed) through developmental levels in standards, rather than age-based grade levels. In a RISC system, students also must meet an acceptable level of performance, but the bar is set higher. To move ahead to the next level in any standards area, a student must demonstrate proficient or better performance on end-of-level assessments—the equivalent of a traditional B letter grade or higher.

In a RISC system, there is agreement about the content students must master, the instructional philosophy that maximizes student learning, and the assessments that will be used, at every developmental level in each standards area, to measure students' growing knowledge and skill. As a result, there is a high degree of consistency in what is taught—teacher to teacher, school to school.

The power of the RISC system is that students do not have to spend 9 months in seventh grade, 9 months in eighth grade, and so on. Instead, they have the flexibility to achieve high school graduation-level performance in each standards area at their own pace. For example, a student may achieve graduation level in one standard at age 12, in another at age 14, and in yet another at age 16; other students may not reach those levels until age 19 or 20. Whether a student completes his or her K–12 education by the equivalent of grade 8, 10, or 12 matters little. What matters are the answers to these questions: Has the student truly learned? Is he or she prepared to succeed, to the fullest extent of the word, in the workplace, in postsecondary education, and in life? Toward this end, school systems that are committed to adopting the RISC Approach to Schooling also commit to applying for and obtaining a state waiver from the Carnegie unit graduation requirement, and instead measure graduation readiness by students' demonstrated proficient or better performance on standards-based assessments.

A growing number of schools or districts in Alaska and in the Lower 48 states have committed to making the transformation to the RISC philosophy and system of education (see www.reinventingschools.org for the latest list of RISC sites). The RISC approach is a fundamentally distinct perspective about what it means to prepare students for success beyond high school—in the workplace, in the global economy, and in life—as they pursue higher education degrees, and as they interact as citizens, at home and abroad. A dramatic change in education, the kind of paradigm shift described in this book, is imperative if the United States is serious about its pledge to provide a world-class education for every child. The kind of deep changes that this shift will require are consistent with second-order change.

Second-Order Change: Shaking Up the Status Quo

As Marzano et al. (1995) state so well, "One of the constants within education is that someone is always trying to change it" (p. 162). Numerous innovations, many of them research-based, have come and gone in education, yet most have failed—not because the innovations themselves were poor, but because those who led the reform process did not consider the dynamics of the change process.

Building on the work of previous education researchers and theorists (specifically, Watzlawick, Weakland, & Fisch, 1974), Marzano (Marzano et al., 1995; Marzano, Waters, & McNulty, 2005) discusses two types of change: first-order and second-order change. In *School Leadership That Works* (2005), Marzano and his colleagues distinguish first-order from second-order change, which they also refer to as incremental versus deep change:

> First-order change is incremental. It can be thought of as the next most obvious step to take in a school or district. Second-order change is anything but incremental. It involves dramatic departures from the expected, both in defining a given problem and in finding a solution. . . . Incremental change fine-tunes the system through a series of small steps that do not depart radically from the past. Deep change alters the system in fundamental ways,

offering a dramatic shift in direction and requiring new ways of thinking and acting. (p. 66)

First-order change means engaging in activities that are essentially variations of what has been done before. Second-order change means engaging in actions that represent significant variations from the past *and* from anticipated future paths—what we think will likely happen in the future.

Second-order change shakes up the status quo and challenges underlying assumptions and beliefs. Relative to education, second-order change equates to a transformation of the primary operating principles, structure, and design of the education system. *To transform* the system "implies a major change in form, nature, or function" (Merriam-Webster, 2008).

Given the deep changes that this shift will require, school leaders who take on the challenge of adopting this standards-based model must be driven by a core commitment to children—in other words, a deep sense of moral purpose.

Commitment and Moral Purpose

At the core of successful second-order change is commitment (Marzano et al., 1995). In this case, successfully making the transformative shift to the standards-based RISC approach occurs as a result of a commitment to children, a "moral direction"—doing what's right for kids, for the sake of our children's future.

People are inspired to become teachers for a variety of reasons—a passion for teaching, a deep love of students, a commitment to the greater good for society, or a core value of service to others, to mention a few. Regardless of what inspired them to join the profession in the first place, teachers share a common moral purpose: a dedication to helping individual students.

At conferences and workshops where the RISC Approach to Schooling and its successful replication are presented, frequently there are individuals in the audience who seem more focused on how the approach will fail rather than the possibilities it offers. In speaking with them, it is clear that some simply cannot yet see how the individualized processes underlying this new philosophy could possibly work; for others the structures and policies of the education system have overshadowed their original sense of purpose.

Instead of being discouraged by this, we are excited. Why? Because those who take on the challenge and embrace the RISC Approach to Schooling will alter the future for so many students for the better.

John Davis, who retired as superintendent of Alaska's Bering Strait School District in June 2007, is one of those who took on the challenge. When he became district superintendent in 1999, people asked him, "What are you going to do with this role now that you have it?" Whatever he was going to do, it was not going to be business as usual:

> My career had spanned 25 years and most likely this would be my last job. Like a couple of wise leaders before me, I asked myself, "Am I going to do something with it? Or am I just going to ride out to retirement?"

> I knew I wanted this last go to make a difference, but I didn't know exactly how to do it until I heard about this approach. The people who developed it were doing what I'd always hoped to do: create a school district that works for all students.

> Over time, we made the same thing happen here. Now our district is one in which whether students are truly learning is more important than teaching our favorite lesson or getting up and doing a good job of entertaining students. So I have the habit of telling people, "It's not about us. It's about students."

There is a vast difference between something that seems like a good idea and something one commits to accomplishing or realizing. This distinction has been studied extensively by a number of education researchers and theorists, most notably Heinz Heckhausen and Julius Kuhl (Heckhausen & Kuhl, 1985, and Heckhausen, 1991, cited in Oettingen, Hönig, & Gollwitzer, 2000) who liken the process of moving from wishes to action to crossing a metaphorical Rubicon.

The phrase *crossing the Rubicon* arose from a historical moment more than 2,000 years ago, in 49 B.C., when Julius Caesar deliberately crossed the Rubicon River into northern Italy with his soldiers to seize power in Rome. As Caesar and his troops crossed the Rubicon, historians tell us he shouted, "The die is now cast!" There was no turning back. Caesar's move precipitated civil war and was a significant factor in the establishment of the Roman Empire.

"Crossing the Rubicon" captures the spirit of committing oneself fully to a potentially risky but inspiring or compelling course of action. Once this commitment has been made, as Marzano et al. (1995) write, individuals shift their attention and intention to making real the commitment:

> No more are their energies devoted to weighing alternatives or considering contingencies. Rather, energies are focused on manifesting the commitment. (p. 168)

This shift in focus from thinking about something or taking a few preliminary steps to engaging in decisive action is eloquently captured in a frequently quoted passage from *The Scottish Himalayan Expedition* (1951) by William H. Murray, one of Scotland's most influential mountain climbing and conservation writers. For months, Murray and his team had thought about the trip and committed themselves to some extent, but when they bought their tickets to sail to Bombay, the entire momentum of the trip shifted dramatically:

> But when I said that nothing had been done I erred in one important matter. We had definitely committed ourselves and were half-way out of our ruts. We had put down our passage money—booked a sailing to Bombay. This may sound too simple, but is great in consequence. Until one is committed there is hesitancy, the chance to draw back, always ineffectiveness. Concerning all acts of initiative (and creation), there is one elementary truth, the ignorance of which kills countless ideas and splendid plans: that the moment one definitely commits oneself, then Providence moves too. All sorts of things occur to help one that would never otherwise have occurred. A whole stream of events issues from the decision, raising in one's favour all manner of unforeseen incidents and meetings and material assistance, which no man could have dreamt would have come his way. (pp. 6–7)

Commitment has a tremendous influence on the effectiveness of human endeavors. It is the fuel that transforms a good idea into an accomplishment, although it does not mean that the path will be easy or simple.

When we look back at the U.S. education system years from now, we will either have a powerfully effective education system that delivers on the shared vision of the U.S. citizenry, or we will have all of our reasons for not having it. The choice is ours.

2

A Journey of Transformation

Leading Questions

1. What are the burning issues and opportunities for improvement in your school or district?

2. Do the educators in your system have regular, open, schoolwide, and districtwide conversations about student achievement?

3. Does your school or district have a shared vision, or are administrators, teachers, parents, and community stakeholders working at cross-purposes?

4. Are you willing to be a leader—among your colleagues, in your school, in your district, or with your fellow board members—in bringing about positive change?

There is a story passed down orally through the ages, generation to generation, about the origin of the name *Chugach*. John F. C. Johnson, an Alaska Native whose family is from the village of Nuchek in Prince William Sound, shares a tale related to him by the late John Klashinoff, who was born in Nuchek in 1906:

> John Klashinoff learned many stories from my grandmother's uncle, Chief Makari (Makarka) Chimovitski, who adopted and raised him and 10 other orphans at a new settlement called Makarka Point. In the early 1900's an epidemic that swept across Alaska claimed John's parents and many others.
>
> As he smoked his pipe and scratched his chin, John was proud to tell me old stories so that the traditions and beliefs of the Chugach would not die, but would live on as it was meant to be. The story is told as follows.

For ages and ages Prince William Sound as it was named by Captain James Cook was covered by a solid sheet of glacier ice that extended over nearly all of the bays and mountains. One day Native hunters were kayaking along the outer shores of the Pacific Ocean, when a man cried out:

"*Chu-ga, Chu-ga* (hurry, hurry).

"Let's go see what that black thing is sticking out of the ice."

So the hunters paddled closer and closer to see what it was. Within a short distance, the hunters could see mountaintops emerging out of the retreating ice. Thus these ocean travelers settled along the ice-free shores of the Sound.

As the seasons changed from year to year, the ice melted rapidly, exposing deep fjords and lagoons that were rich in sea life and provided good beaches to settle on. It was known that life thrived in the areas where the salt and fresh water met.

When the ice retreated, so did the animals. The Chugach people followed the ice and animals deep into the heart of Prince William Sound, where they remain to this very day. (Johnson, 1999)

As we tell this tale of a revolution in American education, we borrow those urgent words from those long-ago ocean adventurers: *Chu-ga, Chu-ga,* hurry, hurry. We have an opportunity to draw on everything we know about how students learn, and what makes schooling effective, to create a system that ensures that every child succeeds in fulfilling his or her highest dreams and abilities. The time is now.

Chugach School District: Seeds of an Education Revolution

Formed in 1975 by the state of Alaska, the Chugach School District is surrounded by the Chugach National Forest and capped by a 300-mile-long stretch of snowy mountains to the north called the Chugach Mountain Range. The name *Chugach* conjures images of this vast area of south central Alaska. It is also the site of the seeds of a revolution in American education.

This is a story of people who did not simply talk about education reform; they actually did it. In 1994, the Chugach School District began to design a radically different approach to educating students, a way of thinking virtually unheard of anywhere in the United States—and those schools and administrators who *had* heard of it were not doing it.

The impetus was the clarity gained from a hard look at student test results and 20 years of historical district data. Ninety percent of the district's students could not read at grade level, and average student achievement in reading, writing, and mathematics on national standardized tests was in the bottom quartile. As in so much of rural Alaska, many students lived in poverty and staff turnover was extremely high.

Over a 5-year period, compelled by a commitment to create a system that would meet the learning needs of *every* student, not just *some* students, administrators and teachers took the district through the eye of the needle of transformation amidst the most challenging academic, social, and geographic conditions. With input from its schools, parents, community members, and business leaders, the district developed standards in 10 content areas; moved away from traditional grade levels to performance levels; developed a new instructional model, assessments, and reporting systems, all of which were aligned with standards; set a higher bar for student achievement; and moved away from Carnegie units to a completely performance-based approach to student progress and graduation.

Leadership was built at all levels of the organization, and the district became a highly energized and focused team working, for the first time, as a whole toward the same goal. District staff put their careers on the line in very real ways. Many times their focus and commitment were tested, but they continued to take risks and face the barrage of dissent for the sake of students.

In a few short years, extraordinary results were realized in the Chugach School District. Most noteworthy:

- Over a 5-year period, average student achievement on the California Achievement Test rose from the bottom quartile to the 72nd percentile.

- The percentage of students participating in college entrance exams rose from 0% to more than 70% by 2000. In the previous history of the district, a period that spanned 20 years, only one student had attended college.

- Between 1995 and 2000, teacher turnover was 12%; in the previous 20-year history of the district, turnover was 55% yearly (National Institute of Standards and Technology [NIST], Baldrige National Quality Program, 2001, pp. xii, 42, xv, 47).

By 2000, the district had become a nationally recognized education leader and a winner of the New American High Schools Award for its innovative, successful whole-school reform effort; soon thereafter, the district was granted the Native American Exemplar Award by the Catching the Dream organization (see www.catchingthedream.org for more information about the organization's awards). In 2001, the district climbed the highest mountain yet when it won the coveted Malcolm Baldrige National Quality Award, the nation's most prestigious award for organizational performance excellence and quality achievement. The Chugach School District was the first organization to win the award as a first-time applicant without winning a state-level performance excellence award, and was also the smallest organization ever to win the award. Since the district won the Baldrige Award in 2001, only three other school districts have received this award.

Alaska's Burning Platform

Alaska. To the average person living in the Lower 48, Alaska brings to mind images of glaciers, oil, salmon, the Northern lights, the midnight sun, miles and miles of untouched wilderness, volcanoes, Mount McKinley, and a sense of cold nearly incomprehensible compared to anything "cold" below the 49th parallel.

What may not be so well-known to the average Lower 48er is the downward personal and social pull experienced by generations of Alaskans of all ages. Alaska's suicide rate is twice that of the national average; unemployment and poverty are serious statewide issues.

In the business world, the term *burning platform* has long been used to indicate a crisis of such magnitude that it forces change. In Alaska, student performance, dropouts, and graduation rates have been of great concern for many years. It was only a matter of time before they reached burning platform proportions.

While cities and states across the country suffer from violence, homelessness, unemployment, cultural and ethnic conflict, gangs, and so on, Alaska's particular scourge is alcohol. Abuse of alcohol is a persistent core problem. This is perhaps both the root and outcome of the unemployment, homelessness, poverty, and scarce economic opportunities that are characteristic of much of rural Alaska. (See Goldsmith, Angvik, Howe, Hill, & Leask, 2004; and see Alaska State Troopers, Alaska Bureau of Alcohol and Drug Enforcement, 2007.)

> Despite the widespread view of Alaska as an idyllic refuge, teenage substance abuse is a considerable social and personal problem there. The rates of abuse in Alaska generally mirror, and in some cases surpass, those of the rest of the nation. The 2003 Youth Risk Behavior survey found that 75.1% of Alaska's high school students had used alcohol at least once, 38.7% reported having had at least one drink in the past 30 days, and 26.5% reported a binge drinking episode (consuming five or more drinks within a few hours) within the past 30 days (Centers for Disease Control, 2004). A 2005 evaluation of results from the same survey that was limited to a sample of students in a Chicago school district found that 74.6% of students had used alcohol at least once; for binge drinking, the percentage was 20.6% (Benbow, 2005, and see State of Alaska, Health and Social Services, n.d.). These statistics suggest that all schools grapple with social issues that put students at risk of failure, regardless of school size or locale.

Numerous studies conducted since the 1960s have documented that alcohol and substance abuse are eroding the social, emotional, mental, and economic fabric of Alaskan communities. For instance, testimony before the Senate Committee on Indian Affairs in 2000 detailed the harsh realities of continuing alcohol abuse in Native communities and its related violence and other social costs (United States Senate Committee on Indian Affairs, 2000). Alaska's Department of Education and Early Development has identified alcohol abuse as "Alaska's #1 health concern" (State of Alaska, Department of Education and Early Development, 2005).

The state has an extremely high incidence—if not the highest incidence—of fetal alcohol syndrome in the United States; for the years 1995–1997, there were 1.5 incidences per 1,000 births, according to the Centers for Disease Control (2002). Fetal alcohol syndrome results in a lifetime of mental, physical, social, and behavioral problems, including mental retardation and learning disabilities. A study conducted between July 2000 and March 2005 for the Alaska Department of Health and Social Services showed that over 80% of 755 individuals tested were diagnosed with some level of organic brain damage resulting from prenatal exposure to alcohol (Information Insights, Inc., 2005).

The impact on students is a persistent and deeply troubling issue that affects Alaskan schools in a very real and personal way. For example, during the 2005–2006 school year, two students in the Bering Strait School District died in alcohol-related deaths in the same week. One student, a 15-year-old riding on the back of a four-wheeler, fell through the ice. The other froze to death walking home late one night.

Alcohol abuse, violence, scarce economic opportunities, and unemployment are all part of an interrelated impact—in every way imaginable—on families, communities, and students on a day-to-day basis. The unfortunate reality is that for many students, working on the day's geometry problem is wholly secondary to simply gathering their thoughts or dealing with the confusion and chaos in their minds from the previous night's family upset.

These issues, experienced by many American youth in urban and smaller cities across the country, are compounded in rural Alaskan villages where harsh weather and stunningly beautiful, yet geographically isolated and challenging living conditions are the norm. Access to most Alaskan villages is extremely limited—and costly. On average, the cost of living is 70% higher in Bush Alaska than in Anchorage. Bad weather can prevent travel for days at a time. Acquisition of supplies is difficult, as everything—mail, groceries, equipment, and so on—must come by plane. School administrators considering any kind of purchase must build in the cost of a roundtrip charter flight, which from Anchorage can cost at least $1,000. Delivering 1 computer or 20, for example, may cost about the same.

To the big-city person living within inches of his neighbor, bombarded by the incessant noise of traffic and 24-hour-a-day bustle, the solitude of Alaskan village life may sound like a heavenly reprieve, and it can be. But solitude can easily turn to loneliness in this state, which remains 85% wilderness and where, on average, there is approximately one square mile per person, by far the lowest population density in the United States (U.S. Census Bureau, 2000b).

Another ongoing Alaskan dynamic is cultural. Of the 683,000-plus people who lived in Alaska as of July 1, 2007 (U.S. Census Bureau, 2007), approximately 16% are Alaska Natives. (For Native population estimates, see State of Alaska, Alaska Department of Labor and Workforce Development, 2006). The Native population is made up of four broad groups: Eskimos, Aleuts, Tlingit, and Athabascan Indians. The Chugach people are of Aleut/Eskimo descent and the primary Native culture in the Prince William Sound region of Alaska (Chugach Alaska Corporation, 2006).

Beginning in the late 1700s, explorers and fur traders immigrated to Alaska in search of sea otter pelts and minerals. A collision of world views resulted. Traditional Native languages and cultures were virtually eradicated in an ongoing effort to indoctrinate Natives into the White Man's way, leading to resentment, division, mistrust, and centuries of impact on the Native peoples. Much of the rift between cultures has been healed over the decades, but traces of this historical conflict linger.

Transformation at the Classroom Level: A Vision for What Is Possible for Individual Students

In 1979, against this background of poor student achievement and geographic and social challenges, then-teacher Rich DeLorenzo, newly graduated from Central Washington University, special education degree in hand, moved to the small Alaskan fishing village of Yakutat, situated at the northern end of the Alaskan Peninsula. For the next 15 years, from Yakutat to Juneau to Port Graham (never straying far geographically, at least in Alaskan terms), Rich discovered how to help students succeed in ways they never had.

Over these years, Rich worked as an individual classroom teacher, essentially on his own, doing what he could to help each one of the students in his classes. As he did, he created the building blocks for what would become a nationally recognized education model that would win the attention not only of educators across the state, but the President of the United States.

The first years of Rich's teaching career were focused on helping special education students and students who had severe emotional disturbances, most of whom had not done well in mainstream classes. The challenges were compounded by the unintended consequences of Public Law 94142, which had been signed into law in 1975. Although the intent of the law (now known as the Individuals with Disabilities Education Act) was good, special education audits turned the focus away from teaching and learning to paperwork and compliance with policies and procedures. Students were labeled and stigmatized. Education no longer seemed focused on helping students learn and grow.

To Rich, the mundane, low-level educational content and instruction these students had been given in the past was horrendous. It was as though no one thought they could do any better. But he saw students differently. It was not enough for him to reach a majority of students. He was committed to reaching every student. He focused his energies on creating an environment in which he could do things for students that no one thought teachers could do.

Over time, through trial and error, and out of a drive to be the best teacher he could be and to do whatever he could to improve the lives of these children, Rich began to develop strategies that helped students for whom finding success in traditional classrooms was most difficult. Several things were key: building relationships with students based on trust, bringing rigor to the learning process, motivating and engaging students by tying learning to their individual passions and dreams, making expectations clear, and giving students a clear roadmap to meet those expectations. What most distinguished Rich's classrooms was that he helped students move from being dependent learners to becoming independent learners engaged deeply in their own success. Over time, students took charge of their own learning.

By 1985, Rich was working as a regular classroom teacher in Juneau, Alaska. Moving to the regular classroom was a startling realization: The education system, which should have been focused on helping individual students succeed, was instead mired in long-standing practices that were largely ineffective, used en masse with students, and not based in research. The traditional learning process was disengaging and unmotivating for most students. Teachers seemed to do the best they could, but they did not know how to differentiate instruction and were not meeting the learning needs of many students. As a result, many students were simply passed along the system, grade level to grade level, teacher to teacher, squeaking by with Ds.

Rich became dedicated to finding a better way of educating every student, one that focused on answering two vital questions: Are we making a difference? Is what we are doing helping students to be successful?

Like many teachers today, teachers in the late 1970s and early 1980s worked almost exclusively in isolation. Rich was no exception. No one asked him what he was doing, and he did not offer an explanation. He was focused on his students and how to help them.

Rich began to seek out best practices and research on effective instruction, motivation, engagement, and learning. His silent partners were Madeline Hunter, Benjamin Bloom, Abraham Maslow, Edward Deming, and a host of other education researchers and philosophers. His practical partners were master teachers, whom he studied and observed in action. One particular teacher who stood out was Bill Cass, with whom Rich taught in 1980 in the small community of Yakutat and who later became principal at Silver Strand School in California's Coronado Unified School District in 2007. What Bill did so well, and what Rich incorporated into his own teaching practices, was twofold: building great relationships with students, and bringing academic rigor to teaching and learning. Everything Rich was learning—from research and theory to best practice—he absorbed, reflected on, and tried out with his students.

Every moment of class time, and every week of the year, was purposeful. For instance, the first 2 weeks of school were spent laying a foundation for the rest of the year. Rich began a dialogue with students that set the tone for their next 9 months together. He engaged students in conversations about learning, what the learning process would look like, and how to set goals. He asked questions such as: What would a perfect class look like? What traits does an excellent teacher demonstrate? What kinds of things does a successful student do? How do you want to be treated? How should you treat others? What are the values and beliefs of a great classroom? What strategies do you need to be a successful learner? Together, the class discussed these issues and others and made decisions. They also determined how they would resolve conflicts, how they would work together in groups, and how they would play together on the playground. Through it all, Rich focused on building relationships with students.

Learning in Rich's classroom involved direct instruction, but classroom application, practice, and simulation, as well as real-life application were also part of the equation. No longer was school simply a matter of textbook, often-redundant learning. The learning process was rigorous and meaningful, but also fun and engaging, so engaging that students often could not stop thinking about learning.

This was new not only for students, but an adjustment for their parents as well. Rich recalls a late night call from a concerned parent.

"Mr. DeLorenzo, Brandon came home today from school. Everything seemed fine. But tonight I caught him in bed with the flashlight working on designs. Is there something wrong at school?"

"Yes, Mrs. Johnson," replied Rich. "Your son is engaged in learning."

School, class lessons, tests, and so on—which students had previously viewed as frustrating, boring, and something to just get through—now were things students looked forward to, things that made them eager to come to school. Even those students who had always had a hard time in school were motivated.

In 1992, Rich accepted a teacher-principal position with Port Graham School, a 30-student K–10 school in the Kenai Peninsula Borough School District, located at the end of the Kenai Peninsula just off the Gulf of Alaska. The cognitive level of the 16 students in Rich's junior high school class ranged from fifth grade to college level. Here he expanded and deepened the tools and processes he had developed with his younger students in Yakutat and Juneau and applied them to older students.

Rather than automatically marching through district-assigned textbooks chapter by chapter, he prioritized topics for the year based on what *students* were interested in learning and worked with students to create learning experiences beyond the classroom. For example, instead of reading the health text and answering the questions at the end of each chapter, the class decided to put on a 4-day health fair and invited other schools to participate. Rich empowered students to be teachers at individual sessions, thereby deepening their own learning, strengthening their leadership skills, and increasing their confidence. Students developed scoring guides. Also, as they had so frequently seen Rich model in their own classrooms, they taught other students essential information and skills, and then created activities that required visiting students to apply and practice what they were learning through role-playing and other activities.

Some of the rewards of the strategies Rich used with his students in Yakutat, Juneau, and Port Graham were immediate: students were motivated and engaged in learning; students worked together, both amongst themselves and with Rich; students experienced success; students had a better sense of themselves; and students who had previously been held back progressed through the grade levels. One of the long-term rewards of Rich's years in teaching, he realized much later, was letters he received from former students thanking him for making learning something to look forward to, for making that kind of difference, and for altering the course of their lives.

The Chugach Journey

Up to this point as an educator, Rich had been trying to impact students in his corner of the world. He virtually never told other teachers what he was doing; he just closed his door and made it happen. But soon others began to take notice. What was going on in this classroom on the shores of Port Graham at the southern tip of the Kenai Peninsula?

Leadership Coalesces Around a Mission: The Possibility of Change at the System Level

One person who noticed was Roger Sampson, who would end up playing one of the most vital roles in the transformation of education that the Chugach School District was about to undertake. The year was 1994 and Roger, president of the Education Commission of the States since July 2007, had just accepted the position of superintendent of Chugach School District. As a long-time principal, Roger was well aware of the problems in the traditional education system and was eager to make dramatic changes, but he was not sure how to go about making the kind of changes that were needed.

Even before his first day on the job, Roger considered Rich DeLorenzo to be the front runner for assistant superintendent, despite the fact that Rich had not yet interviewed for the position. "Rich was strong on instruction," says Roger. "He deeply connected with students. He was a visionary. He was passionate about education, and he was passionate about children."

Rich also had refined a set of tools and processes to teach others to do what he had done in his classrooms. He demonstrated lessons for teachers, modeled how to build assessments aligned with standards, and so on. As Roger put it, "He could see it, articulate it, and the best thing is that he could model it."

Rich and Roger started at the Chugach district on the same day. Prior to that first day, they had no idea of the lay of the land in the district. They had not met the students or visited the district's village schools, although they were well aware of the district's overall poor achievement scores, the widespread drug and alcohol problems, the high rates of poverty, unemployment, and suicide, and the social issues that seemed deeply rooted in the district's communities.

Compounding the problems were the hundreds of miles that lay between each of the school's communities. Many school districts across the United States are as small as the Chugach School District, but none are also so large geographically. The district's 200-plus students are spread across 22,000 square miles of glaciers, mountains, islands, and isolated wilderness that includes most of the Prince William Sound coastline and islands. Some 22,000 square miles is hard to visualize. Imagine an area slightly smaller than Virginia, twice as big as Massachusetts, or about the size of Lake Huron. Now imagine that less than 500 people live in this large expanse of rural geography, and that most of the communities are accessible only by small plane or boat (U.S. Census Bureau, 2000a).

To someone living in New York or Kansas or California, *rural* brings to mind meadows with grazing cows, perhaps a farmhouse perched on the ridge of a nearby hill. In Alaska, *rural* encompasses something wholly different.

Alaskans explain that there are three levels of rural in the state. Level 1 areas are small, somewhat isolated villages connected to a road system with access to an urban hub in 2 to 3 hours. Level 2 areas are more inaccessible. Where a road system is available, access to an urban area translates into close to 20 hours of driving. More often than not, however, Level 2 areas are accessible only by small plane or boat.

Level 3 areas are extremely isolated and rugged in every regard (geography, weather, terrain, and conditions). Most of these areas do not have a septic sewer system or running water. Planes arrive only intermittently, mail is delivered once a week, and in some locations, residents cannot get out for weeks at a time, making these areas the most intensely challenging places to live and work. Moving to one of these villages is a feat in and of itself as your belongings—clothing, household goods, furniture, and so on—must be mailed, a process that can take 2 to 3 weeks.

Rich and Roger were well aware of the tremendous challenges they faced, but they also saw eye to eye about the tremendous opportunity as well. They shared a passion for education and students, as well as what Roger describes as "a commitment to do the right things to help students":

> We were both frustrated with our long careers, at different levels of administration, at not being able to do things we thought were the right things to do. People would say, "We don't have the money," or "That's against board policy," or "That's not the way we do business."

Rich and I said, "Given the chance to be in control and make those decisions, I will put my career on the line to try to do the right things that get the right results."

The two of them began to take the steps to re-create the Chugach School District. They staked their reputations and careers on their decisions, week after week, to make sure it happened, in a way administrators have rarely done.

Whether it was divine timing, happenstance, straightforward vision and planning, or perhaps all of the above, Rich and Roger came together at this point in time as the perfect catalyst for what was about to be the Chugach transformation. These two forward-thinking individuals shared a passion to turn the long-standing education system inside out; they quickly developed a synergy that helped create a new system that worked for every student.

Dawning Realization

A significant moment that escalated the momentum for systemwide change occurred during the first state department of education meeting Rich attended as assistant superintendent. About 30 minutes after the meeting began, Rich realized that people with much more experience than he had and a lot of authority seemed to be caught up in perpetuating the bureaucracy, and students were primarily an afterthought.

Rich became convinced that the strategies and processes he had developed with the students in his classes could be done at a system level. In fact, he realized, change *must* occur at the system level in order to reach every child, and for improvements in student achievement to be sustained over time. In the next moment, he realized, "We can create a system in the Chugach district that makes that kind of difference."

What the Chugach School District had done in the past had not worked, and district leaders knew from studying other reform efforts that a piecemeal approach was not going to work either. What was needed, explained Roger, was a transformation of the entire system; otherwise they would fail like so many other educators before them. They knew that such a transformation could be threatening; they would likely run up against significant resistance along the way. But by transforming the system all at once, rather than in increments, the momentum was on their side, they would be in a stronger place to face resistance to change, and the resulting change would be more likely to be sustained:

> We certainly could have done what most schools that look at reform do: improve one or more pieces of the puzzle: reading, math, and personal skills, for example. But we were all too familiar with the crab pot syndrome, one of the main reasons that well-intended individuals and groups of individuals have made little change in public education.
>
> It's not because they haven't desired it or because they haven't had good ideas. People go along with change until you begin to get on their turf, and then it becomes personal. And when you get on their turf, they shut down. And they are going to pull you back in, like a crab in a pot.
>
> So many people have started off on reform, well intentioned and productive, but the efforts suddenly died and they couldn't figure out why. It's because if you're going to change, you have to commit to changing all of the elements or you're going to get consumed by that resistance and the change won't be deep enough to be sustainable.

As they began to flesh out the specifics of the new approach they were crafting, recalled Roger, they bit off a little at a time—what they thought they could do and do well—and it kept growing and growing:

> There was not a time when we said, "We're going to develop a new model." It was step by step, piece by piece. We didn't think we had "the answer." But we knew we were going to go down this route because it couldn't be worse than where we were going. We were just not going to sit by and do what everybody had been doing for so long and expect different results.

Rich and Roger knew they would need a strong team of educators to carry out the mission to dramatically improve education in the district. Roger emphasized over and over again the level of dedication it was going to take, and that eventually everyone would benefit. Staff members who lacked that level of dedication were told, "This is not the right place for you." The interviewing and hiring process became finely tuned to find talented people who were problem-solvers, who were resilient, and who had a strong moral purpose to do the right thing for students.

Engaging Stakeholders

One of the first steps Rich and Roger took was to engage each of the district's stakeholder groups in developing a collective vision of education in each of the Chugach School District's communities. The deep changes the two leaders were committed to making would succeed only if they grew out of a vision shaped collectively by all stakeholders. This collective purpose was needed to drive the direction of the district in every way, from policy setting and budgeting to instruction and assessment.

Business leaders were the first community group approached. Rich's initial contacts led virtually nowhere. Key decision-makers did not want to meet with district administrators, so Rich turned to the governor's office for leverage. Eventually, leaders of ARCO, General Communications Incorporated, British Petroleum, FedEx, and other businesses recognized statewide agreed to come to the table.

But they did so reluctantly. "Every time we come to a meeting," they said, "nothing happens." Rich and Roger gave them their word that things would be different this time. What set the Chugach group apart was that this was one of the first times that educators did not go to businesses and ask for money. What they sought, instead, was business leaders' advice and expertise.

The meeting was spent asking and answering three questions: What is working? What is not working? What are your recommendations? By the end of the meeting, the room's walls were filled with pages and pages of notes, most of which dealt with what was not working, along with recommendations for correcting weak areas.

Like other business leaders across the United States, the group said that graduates' basic skills were sorely lacking and that their understanding of technology was insufficient for the current workplace. In addition, graduates seemed wholly unprepared for the college application and job interviewing process, let alone the demands of college life and the responsibilities of full-time employment. Finally, they asserted, no one was accountable for results in education. The schooling process needed to be strengthened in each of these areas.

Rich and Roger made a commitment to return with a plan for addressing the group's recommendations. It was a year before they were back knocking at the group's door. During that year, they held a dozen or more meetings with teachers, parents and community members, and students.

As they began to refine their ideas for a new approach to helping students succeed, they continued to ask, "What is it going to take to transform schooling from teachers' perspectives, the community's perspectives, and students' perspectives?"

Confronting the Brutal Facts with Staff

When . . . you start with an honest and diligent effort to determine the truth of the situation, the right decisions often become self-evident. . . . And even if all decisions do not become self-evident, one thing is certain: You absolutely cannot make a series of good decisions without first confronting the brutal facts. (Collins, 2002, p. 70)

One of the next steps was to bring the Chugach staff together, including Rick Schreiber and Wendy Battino, newly married and in their first year of teaching with the district, who would become two of the most central individuals in the refinement, expansion, and replication of the rapidly evolving model of schooling.

In fall of 1995, Wendy and Rick, along with the rest of the Chugach teaching staff—most of whom lived 600–700 miles away—were flown to Anchorage for an intensive 3-day workshop. In order to assess the health of the organization, the team studied 20 years of district data: student achievement results, graduation rates, numbers of students attending college and graduating from college, the teacher attrition rate, and so on—all of the indicators of a high-performance, quality education system.

The Chugach team confronted the "brutal facts" about their students and the challenges they faced as a district. Students could not read, they were not going to college, they were performing in the bottom quartile on standardized national tests, and there were tremendous vocational and economic challenges. Only one conclusion was obvious: The district was failing. As Roger Sampson put it:

> We looked at our students over a 20-year period and we were failing miserably. Our students were failing. I'm not just talking about failing on tests. They were failing at any kind of postsecondary training or vocational training. They were failing at being productive members of their communities or villages. They were totally failing. So we had to ask ourselves, "Are we going to continue to do the same thing over and over and over again? Or are we going to do something different?"

Teachers said that everywhere they looked, the situation was unhealthy. Students were unmotivated. The curriculum was not meaningful; in fact, it was boring. Parents were not involved in schools. The district was losing teachers every year. Family stresses and alcohol abuse were widespread. Schools were not meeting the needs of students, and no plans were in place to attend to the problem.

The team talked about how to turn things around. Rich and Roger asked many questions about instruction, assessment, specific subject areas, and the future of schooling: What do we want education to look like? What are the real issues? What is preventing us from helping students succeed? What are some of the obstacles to high achievement?

The fall 1995 intensive workshop was a crucial laying of groundwork with district staff, particularly teachers, who as students' first point of contact would be the ones to initially implement the process with students—to make it work most effectively on the ground, day by day. Rich and Roger articulated clear goals that would guide the process and created many of the initial tools and processes for teachers. Seeking teachers' advice, guidance, and partnership came out of a deep-seated clarity that the effort would not succeed without them.

As Ann Weaver Hart (1992, cited in Fullan, 1993) notes, when teachers are faced with unfulfilling work conditions and are devalued as professionals, they are unlikely to commit to new initiatives; conversely, "when they see new tasks contributing to quality instruction and core teaching and learning activities, they praise them" (p. 59). This notion—that teacher commitment, shared vision, and the development of a community pay great dividends—is vividly illustrated in Chugach's teacher turnover rate. In 1994, turnover exceeded 50%, reflecting Alaska's high overall teacher and administrator turnover. Between 1995 and 2000, teacher longevity increased significantly; over this 5-year period, turnover was just 12% (NIST, Baldrige, 2001, p. 47).

Pulling in the Community, Even the Skeptics

The next group that district leaders met with was parents, village elders, and other community members. The district's relationship with the community at the time was very poor. Distrust hung in the air.

Community members' perspectives mirrored those of the teachers: Schools were failing, students were failing, and they had no faith that anything was going to change. Why would they? School was at best a tolerable experience for most of them; at worst, a bitter one. Older Native community members recalled an environment in which they were not allowed to speak their language and their culture was suppressed. Although the cultural climate had dramatically changed since those years, still there was a fragile relationship between school and community.

Most parents had an arm's-length relationship with the school; others viewed school with open disdain. One longtime logger in the Icy Bay community, for instance, had grown up in an Alaskan village school where his experiences as a young student were quite negative. Years later, when he brought his third-grade daughter to her first day of school, he stopped on the steps of the school and told one of the teachers that he would allow his daughter to attend, but he would never step foot in the school. "But," he said vehemently, "I *will* come in if I hear any complaints from my daughter."

Parents and community members, like those in other district sites, were highly skeptical—and in some cases downright oppositional—about the Chugach School District's new approach to schooling. During the first months of the 1995–1996 school year, the Chugach team worked to get community members across the district to meetings, many of whom had never been inside the school. They held potlucks, raffles, and student performances; anything and everything to encourage community members to attend meetings. Many times, only one parent showed up.

The Chugach district staff also spent time building relationships, which meant flying out to the villages and staying there, not simply chatting with locals for a few minutes while the plane stayed on the runway and then taking off. Instead, they spent nights in the villages, talking with parents and visiting with families.

By midyear, community members began to see that the district staff was serious about student learning and serious about change. By January of that year, the logger who said he would never set foot in the school folded his 6'2" frame into his daughter's third-grade seat and attended a parent meeting. Soon he was supporting the district's commitment to move away from the traditional A–F grading system to a more rigorous, standards-based approach. He began to stop by school frequently and, before long, offered to teach students tracking and survival skills.

A Shared Vision Emerges

During the 1995–1996 school year, representatives from the district's five school communities came together. Each team considered their site-specific needs and how they were going to be met. The priorities in each community mirrored those in other communities. As a result, district leaders identified five focus areas that reflected the common threads gleaned from cross-district stakeholder input and from business leaders during the previous year:

1. **Basic skills.** Schools had to do a better job of teaching reading, writing, and mathematics—particularly reading.

2. **School-to-life transition.** Students needed opportunities to develop career and life skills to ensure that their transition from the K–12 years to work and life was successful.

3. **Personal, social, and character development.** Students needed strong skills in communication, collaboration, critical thinking, leadership, creative problem solving, and other skills called for in the 21st-century workplace.

4. **Meeting the individual needs of students.** Students' unique abilities and ways of learning needed to be provided for systemically.

5. **Technology.** Students needed to learn to use technology to manage information, solve problems, communicate effectively, and think systemically.

These focus areas were turned into organizational performance goals, which were used to drive the district's strategic planning. Accountability was built into every area of the plan.

Rich, Roger, and other Chugach leaders were dedicated to designing a system that would work—but not just any system. It had to be a system that honored the vision that parents, business leaders, village elders, and other stakeholders had for their children.

Using the districtwide shared vision and organizational goals, teams of teachers came together during the 1995–1996 school year to develop standards. The standards-writing process was particularly challenging since, unlike today, Alaska (like other Western states at the time) did not have state standards in place.

Over the next 2 years, the teams developed standards in 10 areas: mathematics, reading, writing, science, social sciences, technology, service learning, career development, cultural awareness and expression, and personal/social/health development. Teams of district leaders then used a backwards design process to build developmental levels—continuums of learning—for each standards area, from kindergarten through grade 12, to serve as a continuum of student progress toward graduation. They asked themselves, "What knowledge and skills should our graduates have mastered? What personal and social skills do they need?" The next step was the thoughtful construction of aligned assessments for each developmental level in each of the 10 standards areas.

During this time, the Chugach team also developed a new four-strand instructional model that incorporated traditional drill and practice, but also classroom application, interactive simulation, and real-life connection to engage students and provide deeper pathways to learning. One of the key outcomes of the critical thinking that went into developing the new instructional model was the creation of Anchorage House, a residential program designed to give students opportunities to practice the team-building, career-development, and employability skills they were learning in school in a real-world, urban environment.

Validation

In 1996, *A Comprehensive Guide to Designing Standards-Based Districts, Schools, and Classrooms,* by Bob Marzano and John Kendall, was published by the Association for Supervision and Curriculum Development. The Chugach process had been in place for 2 years at that point.

As Rich read the book, he realized that one chapter in particular spoke to precisely what Chugach had been doing. The chapter described four approaches districts could take to incorporate standards. The fourth approach, "Reporting on Individual Standards," was broken down into four models, the last of which Marzano and Kendall called the *nongraded, standards-based approach.*

Marzano and Kendall's description of this approach validated every-thing the Chugach team was doing. Under the nongraded, standards-based approach, there are no grade levels and students work on specific standards at their own pace. The model allows for and builds on students' differing interests and development across subject areas, yet the school or district is standards-based: students must demonstrate competence in specific standards before they can pass from one grade to the next, or one level of schooling to the next. One paragraph in that section, and one line in par-ticular, jumped out at Rich:

> Although the logic of this model is strong, it is very difficult to implement because of the massive changes it requires in schedul-ing, assessment, reporting, and resource association. *It is probably*

for this reason that no school or district we are aware of has seriously attempted to implement this model [italics added]. (pp. 242–243)

When Rich read that line, he called Bob Marzano at his Colorado office in hopes that Bob would be willing to review Chugach's processes and offer more suggestions and recommendations. Bob's reaction was like a slap in the face, says Rich. "He didn't see how we could be doing what we were doing. To say I was disappointed would be putting it nicely."

Over the next couple of years, Bob heard more about what Chugach was doing and began to follow the district team's work. As he studied their innovations and their results, he recalls that he realized, "this was the real deal." In 2003, he was invited to speak at a RISC Summer Institute in Alaska where he stood in front of a roomful of Rich's peers, spoke about the enormous value of the work the district was undertaking, and then publicly apologized to Rich.

"Building the Plane as We're Flying It"

Early successes within the first 2 years of the reform process were encouraging and validated that they were on the right road. Then they started to question other aspects of the traditional education system. If *this* piece is broken, what else is broken? As they continued to develop new tools and processes, teachers used them in their classrooms.

Bob Crumley, then assessment coordinator for the Chugach School District and district superintendent since 2005, frequently said, "We're building the plane as we're flying it," a sentiment that became a mantra for teachers and administrators alike. The saying captured the sense of constant day-to-day refinement and improvement. Everyone knew they were in uncharted waters. They were taking the best available information and guidance from research, applying what they were learning and continually improving.

The majority of the Chugach staff believed in what they were doing, saw already that it made sense, and were excited to make it happen. They knew they were flying the plane as they were building it, but the relative uncertainty only inspired them to move faster. Rich says this was largely the reason that the district saw results sooner than they might have otherwise.

The 1996–1997 school year was one of transition and great change. The district's standards were revised and improved, and a dual report card was instituted. Parents still wanted grades, and Roger and Rich were not sure if the district should jump 100% into a performance-based approach in all 10 standards areas. But by midyear, it was clear that they could straddle the fence no longer. It was sink or swim; they had to move forward.

For the first time in the history of the district, students who did not demonstrate at least a proficient level of performance in all 10 standards areas—meaning, essentially, earning a B at the end of every level in every standards area—would not graduate. There was tremendous resistance from high school students and their parents. In fact, the opposition was like hitting a brick wall. The reaction was surprising since students and parents had been involved in early community meetings about the new approach and had given their feedback.

The problem was that Roger and Rich had not involved students and parents deeply enough. Most important, students and parents were not part of the process of designing the new graduation requirements and did not fully realize what all of it would mean in practice. As a result, what previously sounded like a great idea now looked like too much work. Why should students be held back when everyone else had graduated so easily in the past?

Realizing their mistake in not deeply involving students, the Chugach team spent a great deal of time coaching students to help them understand, "We are going to hold the line. Here is what it is going to take to graduate."

The commitment to high standards began to permeate other areas of the Chugach system. Teachers and administrators were demanding that students demonstrate mastery before they could move forward. Yet, they realized, they were not demanding the same level of excellence from themselves. As a result, in 1997 the district instituted a significant change when its evaluation tools for teachers, administrators, and board members became performance-based.

Faculty pay was now tied to faculty and staff goals and to student advancement across developmental levels. The two-tiered program, providing individual and districtwide performance-based pay, began to be an additional incentive for continuing to grow a system of excellence (NIST, Baldrige, 2001). Everyone began to take a 360-degree view of evaluation; whatever was evaluated regarding students was applied to everyone else involved in the system. If it benefited students, it should benefit everyone else as well. To facilitate the kind of ongoing learning and development that was a match for the district's new goals, 30 days of inservice became the new standard for professional development in the district, essentially doubling the amount of time most districts devote to staff training and development (NIST, Baldrige, 2001).

By the summer of 1997, 3 years into the transformation process, the district's standards had been revised in 10 content areas and aligned assessments were being developed for each developmental level in each standards area. Teachers and staff were excited and energized as they struggled through the process. The staff taught all day and then spent many long nights after school and on weekends to develop assessments aligned with the district's standards. It was an intense and dedicated time mentally, emotionally, and timewise. The lights in the school were on 24 hours a day. The message to the community was clear: "Teachers are working late. These people are serious."

By the following year, 1997–1998, district assessments were in place in reading, writing, and mathematics. Initially, parents, like everyone else, were only partially sold on the new approach, but that changed once assessments were in place. Parents realized that students would have to *prove* that they knew the standards.

This was also the year the district applied for and received a waiver from the Alaska Department of Education and Early Development to forego traditional Carnegie units, or credits, as graduation requirements and instead use students' demonstrated performance on graduation-level district assessments. The waiver was granted, putting into place a critical component of the system and opening the way for the district to formally and informally measure student results through a system of multiple standards-based assessments. No longer would student progress be measured by how long a student sat in his or her seat year after year. Now students had to demonstrate a proficient level of performance on multiple assessments in all 10 of the district's standards areas in order to graduate.

The waiver empowered the district to make its new direction stick. The district had a "5-year lease," so to speak; in 5 years, the new approach would work or the district would go back to the old system. In 5 years, they did not go back; instead, the Chugach staff brought along other districts that wanted to do the same thing. Says Debbie Treece, Quality Schools Coordinator for the district, "I don't think the state board ever envisioned that that's where we were heading."

Results

One of the first results realized in the Chugach School District was a rise in reading test scores. Teachers had continued to get better and better at teaching reading, diagnosing gaps in knowledge and skill, and designing and implementing intervention strategies.

Growth in student achievement in reading—as well as language, math, and spelling—was spectacular, as shown in Figure 2.1. Over a 5-year period, average student achievement on the California Achievement Test (CAT) rose from the 28th percentile to the 71st percentile in reading; in math, from the 54th to the 78th percentile; and in language arts, from the 26th to the 72nd percentile. In 2000, the first year of Alaska's High School Qualifying and Benchmark Exams, 75 to 80% of Chugach students in all grades performed better than the Alaska statewide average (NIST, Baldrige, 2001).

The results were empowering in many ways. For one, students were gaining ownership of their education. Instead of thinking, "What's the teacher going to give me?" or "I'm going to just fail the test and that's okay because that will be over and I'll go on to something new," everyone's perspective was, "We are going to keep working on this until every student has reached mastery and then move forward." Michele Totemoff, one of the first graduates through the Chugach district's new system, remarked in her graduation speech, "I learned more in my last year than in all the previous years of school."

Figure 2.1: Chugach School District CAT Results, 1994–1999

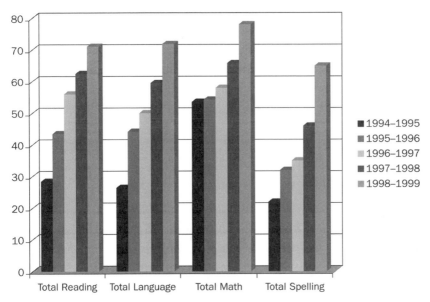

Note: All scores are expressed as national percentiles.

Source: NIST, Baldrige National Quality Program, 2001, p. 41.

Scouts: A Team of Dedicated Individuals

It might be said that with any discovery, paradigm shift, or radical transformation in a system, there are scouts, pioneers, and settlers. The Chugach team members were the scouts. Most traditional educators are settlers. Scouts head out, blaze a trail, and prepare the way. When it is safe, the settlers move into the new area. Being a scout during this time was frustrating. No one had tried the systemic approach, and no one was there to guide the team. As they would so often remark later, they were not only on the cutting edge, but the bleeding edge.

Chugach leaders were not content simply to tweak an obsolete system by making changes in scheduling, attendance policies, or the curriculum adoption process. Instead, over time they entirely redesigned many of the previously unquestioned aspects of schooling that were preventing students and teachers from being successful, which meant challenging state and federal regulations and initiating new policies that would have the greatest impact. In a few short years, district leaders had instituted a number of fundamental changes in the district's education system. They most notably:

- Adopted a standards-based grading system
- Shifted from measuring students' progress by seat time to measuring it by demonstrated performance on standards-based assessments—and in the process received a state waiver from Carnegie unit requirements
- Created a performance-based pay system for teachers
- Dramatically expanded the number of in-service days

The development of the Chugach team—and the dramatic changes the district brought about—began with a team of scouts: dedicated people who brought a wealth of talents and commitment.

One of the core strengths of the Chugach team was their dedication to stay on the journey together, inside and outside of the regular school day and year, which had a tremendous impact on the district's ability to ramp up quickly. People willingly gave their personal time after school, before school, in the evenings, on the weekends—whatever it took—because they were in it for the students no matter the cost. Because they believed in the vision and saw how it could be realized, no one watched the clock or kept track of the hours. For instance, one summer, the team traveled to a Montana camp for an intensive 10 days of work. Staff members willingly gave up their summer time to become better reading teachers. Every teacher, K–12, learned to teach reading. Those were the kind of people who were involved in this district.

Winning the Baldrige Award: A Cinderella Story

In 1999, Roger Sampson retired from the Chugach School District and Rich DeLorenzo became superintendent. One thing that infuriated Rich and other Chugach leaders was that people thought they were "cooking" the district's test scores. Rich set out to find the most rigorous validation that they had done it the right way so no one could question their results.

What We Did Right; What We Did Wrong

With Rich DeLorenzo

With the creation of this new model of schooling, Chugach had waded into uncharted territory; as with any endeavor of this magnitude, there were lessons to be learned along the way. In the 1997–1998 school year, the second year of the initiative, the Chugach team began to revise the shared vision. Students, who initially had not been fully involved in the vision's creation, began to attend communitywide meetings and facilitate discussions. This delayed student involvement meant that ownership of the initiative, too, was delayed.

This was true not only for students, but for other stakeholders as well. The team initially did not include parents of home-schooled children in the shared vision process. Although district leaders eventually did complete that process with these parents, they essentially did the process twice—once with the originally identified group of stakeholders, and once with home-schooling parents—which took twice as long and cost twice as much in staff and financial resources.

The team's focus—the focus of the entire initiative—was the right one. What Chugach started was a student-centered revolution in which children were not simply passive recipients of knowledge, but drivers of the process. This idea, however, was not made entirely clear in the early stages of the program. Given the importance of relationship building and commitment to the success of these changes, the team realized, it was critically important to spend time in the district's communities, ensuring that teachers, parents, students, and community members truly supported and owned the standards identified during the shared vision process—that these standards were not viewed simply as something administrators had developed, but something that everyone supported.

The search led him to the Malcolm Baldrige National Quality Award, "the nation's only Presidential award for quality and organizational performance excellence," recognized as a standard of excellence in the business world to "help U.S. organizations achieve world-class quality" (National Institute of Standards and Technology, 2004). Although the award itself would be a big win for the district, what Rich really wanted was the Baldrige feedback report to confirm the district's tools and processes, to validate the district's results, and to learn what they could do better.

The Baldrige Award, named for Malcolm Baldrige, secretary of commerce from 1981 until his death in 1987, is presented by the President of the United States to businesses, educational institutions, and healthcare organizations that apply and are judged to be outstanding in seven areas:

1. Leadership

2. Strategic planning

3. Customer and market focus

4. Measurement, analysis, and knowledge management

5. Human resource focus

6. Process management

7. Results

The award is managed by the U.S. Commerce Department's National Institute of Standards and Technology (NIST) "in close cooperation with the private sector" (NIST, 2007). The award was established by Congress in 1987, when it was becoming more and more clear that "quality was no longer an option for American companies but a necessity for doing business in an ever expanding, and more demanding, competitive world market" (NIST, 2007).

There are several stages of the Baldrige award process. Along the way, Baldrige judges convene to evaluate the merits of the applicants:

- Stage 1: Independent review

- Stage 2: Consensus review

- Stage 3: Site visit review

- Review and recommend award recipients

To support and help identify potential award applicants and encourage the use of the Baldrige performance criteria, numerous state and local affiliated award programs have been established across the country (NIST,

2006). The road to the national award is a long-term, intensive process that typically means winning a state award before applying for the national award. In some states, there are different tiers to the award (such as bronze, silver, and gold), each of which involves an in-depth application and review process for applicants to navigate. Organizations that ultimately achieve the gold level, after years of moving through the tiers, may choose to apply for the national Baldrige Award.

Chugach's Cinderella story began in 1999. Since Alaska had no state performance excellence award at the time, Rich was invited to travel to Texas to be trained as an examiner for the Texas Quality Award (now called the Texas Award for Performance Excellence). As he sat through the training, he realized there were elements the Chugach team was doing well and others they could strengthen. He also became inspired to submit an application for the national Baldrige award on the district's behalf.

The odds were against them. An experienced lead trainer for the Texas Quality Award, and someone who had coached others in their quality journey, cautioned Rich that this journey would take years, if not decades. Nonetheless, Rich invited her to fly to Alaska to objectively assess the Chugach process. After 3 days of careful review of everything Chugach was doing, astounded by the depth of the district's data, she told the team that they might have what it takes to receive a site visit.

When Rich returned to Alaska, he met with the staff and explained what it was going to take to apply for the national award. The average group of people would have quit many times along the way, but not the Chugach team. This was another critical point where they could have given up, but they were too committed to validating everything they had accomplished with and for students; they would not turn back.

Many long nights and weekends were spent during the 10-month application writing process gathering data and fine-tuning the district's application. Along the way, the team found gaps in what they were doing, all of which they used to keep improving their approach even while they continued to write the Baldrige application. In fall 2001, the Chugach School District submitted its application with the goal of being granted a site visit. Over the ensuing weeks, a team of Baldrige examiners traveled to Alaska and spent hundreds of hours interviewing Chugach administrators and staff, visiting classrooms, and scrutinizing the district's processes, innovations, and results.

The Super Bowl of Education

In late 2001, Rich recalls, he was speaking at a conference in Anchorage. During a break, his cell phone rang and a woman said, "Please hold for Secretary Evans." The next voice said, "This is Secretary of Commerce Don Evans. Congratulations. You did a heck of a job. You just won the Baldrige Award in education."

Standing in the hallway, Rich was so stunned that he virtually hung up on Secretary Evans. The Chugach School District, the little district that virtually no one had heard of, had won the Malcolm Baldrige National Quality Award, the most prestigious and rigorous award for excellence in the United States.

Winning the award meant that Chugach representatives would travel to Washington DC to accept the award, which would be presented by President George W. Bush. Nathaniel Moore, a 16-year-old sophomore at Chugach's Whittier Community School, asked Rich if he could play some kind of role in the celebration. Immediately Rich thought of the Baldrige acceptance speech, which in the history of the award always had been given by the CEO of the winning organization. What more fitting example of Chugach's focus on students, Rich thought, than to have a student represent the district in this key way.

It took some convincing, but eventually NIST officials gave their approval. On March 7, 2002, Nathaniel delivered the speech to a roomful of educators, senators, education and policy leaders, President Bush, and Chugach guests, including his parents, who had traveled from Alaska to be part of the event.

After the awards ceremony, Nathaniel met with President Bush one on one. Here was a 16-year-old student from Alaska, representing his fellow students, taking part in a very visible way in the Chugach School District receiving the highest award in the country for quality.

> "These achievements definitely did not happen overnight. . . .
> It takes dedication, hard work, and a large amount of patience
> to accomplish something like this. In addition to a very
> dedicated staff, it also takes hard work from the students. A
> student can no longer slide by with a D average on his or her
> report card. Students in our district have shown that, with clear
> relevant expectations, they are more likely to succeed. . . .
>
> "From my perspective, this system has challenged me
> unlike the traditional system. My standing here before you is
> testimony to this. I am the one responsible for my education.
> With my district's standards, I have a better knowledge of
> what I need to succeed, not only in school, but also in life."
>
> —Nathaniel Moore, Student, Chugach School District
> Baldrige Awards Ceremony Speech
> March 2002, Washington, DC
>
> *Source:* National Institute of Standards and Technology (2002).

As word began to spread about the Chugach School District's successes, other districts and schools expressed interest in implementing the model, and the Chugach team began to take a leadership role in guiding others. As they did, it became clear that a separate organization was needed to lead this work so that district teachers and staff could continue to focus on serving their own students. Efforts to replicate Chugach's successes are discussed in chapter 4. This chapter discusses the beginning of the Re-Inventing Schools Coalition (RISC), and describes the essential elements of the RISC Approach to Schooling.

The Genesis of RISC

In 2002, while still superintendent for the Chugach School District, Rich DeLorenzo established the Re-Inventing Schools Coalition as a nonprofit organization, along with Wendy Battino and Rick Schreiber (who in time would lead the organization's work). Before long, a diverse board of directors was in place, working side by side with the small RISC staff. The processes, tools, and systems of change that had been developed in the Chugach School District were refined, expanded, reconstituted, and formalized into what would ultimately be known as the RISC Approach to Schooling.

The name RISC was chosen deliberately. Schools and districts that would adopt the RISC model would take risks in transitioning to a system fundamentally distinct from the one that was deeply ingrained in U.S. culture.

The RISC organization was created to help address requests from other organizations, and to garner additional support for the standards-based approach to keep the movement alive. Chugach leaders were doing things that other educators had not done; in effect, they were changing the education paradigm. If the approach was corrupted or the movement failed, DeLorenzo reasoned, what the Chugach School District was doing would likely collapse as well; there would be too much external pressure to go back to business as usual. An equally important priority was to ensure that the model was replicated with fidelity. It was clear that the right thing to do for Chugach's students was the right thing to do for *all* students. The coalition's founders could not, in good conscience, simply sit back and revel in Chugach's success and accolades. They were driven to do what they could to help make the model available to other schools and districts—and therefore all students—nationwide.

The Re-Inventing Schools Coalition soon caught the attention of the Bill & Melinda Gates Foundation, which provided generous funding on three separate occasions to support the coalition's efforts. Two of these grants were given to support other Alaska school districts in reinventing their school systems with equity, in terms of all students learning, and quality, in terms of constantly improving each system. The third grant was provided for leadership training to support the model's implementation. With this funding in hand, RISC has been able to assist numerous schools and districts committed to creating an education system that prepares every student to succeed in life, work, and post-secondary pursuits. The Bill & Melinda Gates Foundation's commitment to make this kind of difference has significantly elevated RISC's ability to reinvent our education system, giving hope to thousands of students in Alaska and across the United States.

3

The RISC Approach to Schooling

Leading Questions

1. Is there room for innovation in your school or district?

2. Does your school or district have organizational goals? Do you know what they are?

3. As an educator in your system, is there accountability for what you do?

4. What are your thoughts about the knowledge and skills students should master before they are granted a high school diploma? What should a confident, prepared high school graduate know and be able to do?

5. What does it look like in your system when a student masters these skills and this knowledge early?

6. Are teachers in the system using standards in their day-to-day instruction? If so, how are they using them?

7. Does instruction flow from standards, or is instruction based solely on textbooks?

8. Are students keeping track of their own progress on standards?

9. Does your assessment and grading system accurately reflect students' relative strengths and weaknesses?

The RISC Approach to Schooling is an integrated standards-based system of education that represents a synthesis of research and best practice about high-performing organizations, educational excellence, the characteristics of effective schools, and fundamentals of human learning, engagement, and motivation. It is fair to say that this model is the first organized, sustainable attempt to use a systems approach to empower students to have a say in what they learn and how they learn—both independently and with teacher guidance and direction—and, as a result, take achievement to new levels.

The individual components that make up the RISC model are not new. What *is* new is the way in which they come together to create a coherent, aligned system. Figure 3.1 highlights the key distinctions between a traditional education system and a RISC system.

Figure 3.1: Traditional System Versus RISC System

	Traditional System	**RISC System**
Standards and Curriculum	No school or district standards are in place; however, teachers may be aware of state standards or standards developed by professional subject-matter organizations. Students move through the curriculum, grade level to grade level, in age-similar groups.	Specific, clear school or district standards are identified in academic and cross-disciplinary areas. Developmental levels have been articulated in each standards area. There is a seamless continuum of learning, K–12, if not K–16. Students move through the levels at their own pace.
Instruction, Assessment, and Reporting	Instruction, assessment, and reporting are not aligned. Instruction is driven primarily by textbooks and external assessments.	Instruction, assessment, and reporting systems are aligned with and flow from standards.
Assessments	Student performance is measured primarily by required state assessments in core areas.	The emphasis is on frequent classroom assessment in every content area at each developmental level, as the individual student is ready. Student performance also is measured by required state assessments in core areas.
Grading	There is a traditional A, B, C, D, F grading system where what these grades mean is often unclear and inconsistent from teacher to teacher.	Rubrics describe in behavioral terms what levels of student performance (for example, emerging, developing, proficient, advanced) look like. Where A–F grades are used, there is clarity and consistency among teachers.

Figure 3.1: Traditional System Versus RISC System *(continued)*

	Traditional System	**RISC System**
Minimum Grade to Move Ahead	D or D–	Students must be proficient, which is roughly equivalent to a B grade. The RISC grading approach can be described as "A, B, or try again."
GPA	.00 to 4.0	3.0 to 4.0
Report Cards	Traditional report cards list courses with grades. Students' progress on a few core standards also may be recognized.	Report cards describe students' progress in mastering the developmental levels in each standards area.
Graduation	Graduation is achieved by seat time: Students graduate when they have attained the required number of Carnegie unit credits (typically, 20–25). Board policy focuses on credits.	Graduation is achieved by performance: Students graduate when they demonstrate proficient or advanced performance at the graduation level in all standards areas, regardless of how many hours they have spent in their seats. Board policy focuses on graduation by performance.

The RISC Approach to Schooling is focused on bringing about systemic change using research-based methods in four interrelated components: standards-based design, shared vision, leadership, and continuous improvement (see Figure 3.2 on page 62). At the heart of the RISC model are principles about students and learning. Among these is the conviction that all students can and will learn. Second, students are individuals who, for a variety of reasons, learn at different rates; therefore, their progress, and ultimately graduation, should be measured by performance rather than time. Third, when students are engaged in learning, take ownership of their education, and are rewarded for achievement and accomplishment (rather than the seat time they earn), learning becomes an opportunity—and student achievement reaches new heights.

Figure 3.2: The RISC Approach to Schooling

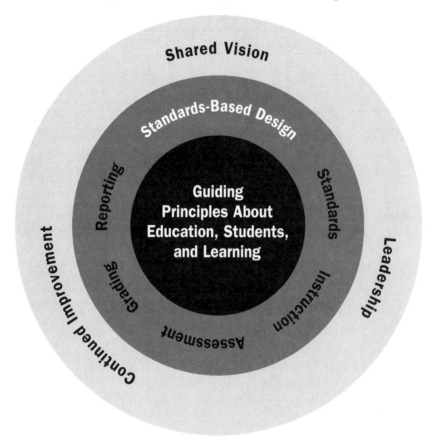

A Tight-Loose System: Optimizing Innovation

In a traditional system, there is a great deal of subjectivity and inconsistency. Expectations for student achievement—even among teachers of the same grade level and/or content area—tend to differ greatly and be unclear. Teachers essentially are engaged in private practice and their expectations for students often are not shared. The content of courses, although essentially set by the curriculum, is not always followed faithfully and, more important, may not be assessed consistently. For instance, what does it mean to pass Algebra I in one class versus another? Does a student have to pass 100 of the 140 lessons in the textbook? 120? Or is it enough to show up to class and have a good attitude? In addition, in a traditional system, what students learn and how well they learn are largely dependent on what teachers teach and how well they teach.

In a RISC system, conversely, expectations are clear and consistent. One of the great advantages of a school that is truly standards based is that students know exactly what they are to learn. The mystery is taken away. No longer do they need to guess or wonder. Students and teachers alike know what students are expected to learn and how student progress will be assessed.

A RISC system can be described as a *tight-loose system*, the optimal system for innovation. Shared goals and expectations for students are tight, but there is significant room for instructional innovation and creativity. The tight aspects of the system mean that RISC teachers and administrators are accountable for student learning and there is agreement about all of the key components. Specifically, there is agreement about the following:

- What students are expected to learn at each developmental level in each standards area

- An instructional model emphasizing application that promotes the highest level of learning

- The rubrics or scoring guides, which all teachers will use, that describe in behavioral terms what various levels of student performance look like

- The common assessments that will be used to gauge students' understanding and application of content knowledge and skills

- The clear reporting processes that everyone will use

The RISC Approach to Schooling aims to create systems that ensure that *all* students have access to great teaching. This outcome is realized in part through shared agreement about the above core elements of a RISC system. This outcome is also realized by a commitment at the organizational level to ensure that the content the school or district says should be addressed at specific developmental levels—in other words, what students are expected to learn—is the same as the content that is delivered by teachers, which is the same as what students actually learn. This distinction, first conceptualized for the Second International Mathematics Study, is what education researchers (Travers & Westbury, 1989, cited in Martin & Kelly, 1996) describe as the *intended curriculum* versus the *implemented curriculum* versus the *attained curriculum*. This distinction is an essential component of what Robert Marzano (2003) calls "a guaranteed and viable currriculum" (p. 22). Marzano synthesized 35 years of research about effective schooling and identified 11 factors that positively impact student achievement, regardless of social, home, and personal factors and other aspects of students' background. Of these 11 factors, Marzano found that providing a guaranteed and viable curriculum has the most impact on student achievement.

As Marzano notes, most people are surprised to learn that what schools and districts intend to teach can vary greatly from what teachers actually teach and what students actually learn. This discrepancy arises largely because of the sheer number of topics teachers are expected to teach and the relatively limited amount of time available for instruction. These inter-related issues compel teachers to unsystematically make decisions about what they will teach, and what they will not.

The number of specific dimensions or pieces of knowledge that teachers must teach—what Marzano (2006) calls *measurement topics*—is of concern in every school or district organized around standards. Like other schools and districts in which academic standards are the centerpiece of the educational process, RISC schools and districts certainly must make decisions about the content that will be taught. However, the degree to which teachers make individual, potentially unsystematic and inconsistent decisions about what to teach is minimized to some extent in RISC settings for two reasons. First, in RISC schools and districts, teachers and administrators come together in advance to make decisions about what specifically will be taught to students and when. As a result, there is a depth of staff ownership and commitment that is lacking in most schools and districts. Second, in RISC school systems, there is a constant awareness of the need to ensure that required content *can* be taught in the time available for instruction, a conversation that is revisited on a frequent basis.

The need to deliver consistent content, and other tight aspects of a RISC system, does not mean that teacher creativity and leadership are compromised; quite the contrary. In fact, teachers have a significant amount of freedom and flexibility. This "loose" aspect of the RISC system means that teachers have a great deal of leeway in:

- The kinds of lessons and learning activities they design for students

- The innovative ways in which they tap into individual students' passions, interests, and skills

- How they lay out and organize their classrooms

- How they inspire students to learn to higher and higher levels

Flexibility and creativity are fostered and realized in RISC systems in part through a professional atmosphere of collegiality, trust, collaboration, and ongoing learning, what is often called a *professional learning community* —oriented around a shared commitment to the success of every student— that encourages teachers to develop and implement new ideas, including ideas and approaches that might be outside the norm; share strategies with their colleagues; succeed *and* fail, and keep learning.

"It used to *look* good in the grade system. Who knows what students were really learning, but they were moved ahead as long as they had a D average. The old system looks disappointing compared to the RISC system. Nothing was very well planned out or carried through in the past. The standards-based system shows us just how sloppy our schools had become."

—Ben Bromiley, Student, Newhalen School
Lake and Peninsula School District, Alaska

To illustrate the differences between a RISC standards- and performance-based system and a traditional system, consider two students: Emma, a student in a RISC school, and Jake, a student in a traditional, non-standards-based school.

In Emma's school, teachers frequently and regularly assess students' knowledge and skill. From the beginning of the school year, Emma's progress is assessed in numerous ways in all of the standards areas she is studying. By January, she has demonstrated proficient or advanced performance on end-of-level assessments in four standards areas (math, history, geography, and technology). She takes on more challenging content in these areas right away, well before the end of the academic year.

In the traditional school that Jake attends, teachers have standards posted on the walls of the classrooms but there are no regular assessments tied to those standards to determine how students are progressing in meeting them. The only classroom assessments given are those provided at the end of each chapter in the textbooks his teachers are using—textbooks that for the most part are only marginally related to the standards posted around the school. Jake earns straight As in all of his courses and advances to the next grade level at the end of the school year. For him, the school year was somewhat challenging in two subject areas (science and English literature), but in every other class he felt as though he had to wait for everyone else to catch up. He knew he was ready to take on more advanced content well before the end of the school year, but he had to wait until the following school year to move ahead academically.

School is relatively easy, although frustrating for Jake, our hypothetical student. Schooling is equally frustrating—and detrimental—for students who struggle to keep up. Despite the potential social benefits of moving students ahead with their age peers, it is a disservice to students to move them to eighth grade, for example, when they barely know the content specified for seventh grade. Students who may have struggled with aspects of the seventh-grade content will continue to struggle in eighth grade, falling farther and farther behind. In addition, across grade levels, there is much repetition of information that students have already learned. The result is that the time students spend in school is used inefficiently and ineffectively. Few organizations would expect each of their employees to complete the same tasks, on the same level, at the same time. Similarly, students need a system that accounts for and is geared toward their differences as individuals.

What a RISC System Looks Like

The philosophy and orientation to learning that underlie the RISC approach manifest in practical, visible ways in RISC systems. On an average day, visitors to a RISC school are likely to be treated to a tour by one of a number of student leaders. In some regards, the school looks like any other school: students in classes, students studying in small groups, and one or two sullen-faced students, clearly in some kind of detention, sitting by the principal's office doing class work.

But beneath those similarities are key differences. There are no bells signaling the end of class, and students have enough flexibility that they could be in the library studying or conducting research for an upcoming project, in a classroom working with a teacher, or out in the community engaged in a service project.

Teaching in a RISC school is going on all the time, not just within the minutes of a designated class period. For instance, as students and teachers are lined up together for lunch, they are talking and learning. If we were to listen in on the conversation, it would be clear that students are quite knowledgeable about what they need to learn to progress to the next level in each content area and what they have to do to show they have learned it. Leaving the lunchroom and walking down the hall, we notice that even the hallway walls differ from most schools. Artwork is posted here and there, but lists of standards, scoring guides, and student projects, papers, and other academic work dominate the spaces.

The classroom is another place where the unique dynamics of the RISC approach show up quite visibly. Students are working together not by age, but rather by the content they are learning. They are working in pairs, in small or large groups, and individually. The teacher may be observing a pair of students working together on a project, providing direct instruction to a small group of students, or coaching a student one on one.

Even at a young age, students are very visible partners and co-creators in getting the most out of their education. They are meeting with their teachers to talk about specific learning activities—and, over time, to co-design learning activities and make decisions about the kinds of assessments and related rubrics or scoring guides that will be used to measure their depth of understanding and skill. Students are up, out of their seats, interacting with their teachers and with one another, and finding real-life connections for what they are learning and *why* they are learning it. In a sense, a RISC classroom might be described as "controlled, deliberate chaos."

How and Why It Works

"With the traditional system of education, there is no target; there is no specific set of content a student must truly learn before moving on. If a child is not doing well for whatever reason, we say, 'Well, Johnny tries really hard, so we'll give him an A.' But Johnny hasn't learned anything. He's moved up, but he is in more trouble now than he was the previous year.

"With the standards- and performance-based system, that doesn't happen because we're assessing all the time to find out where Johnny is, and, if he needs extra help, he gets extra help now, not 6 months down the line when it's too late and he's 6 months behind everybody else.

"On the other hand, if something is especially easy for Johnny, he isn't held back by the rest of the class; he goes on to the next level of achievement. There are no grade levels, only levels of achievement. And some children may go through three levels in one school year; others, sitting in the same classroom, may go through one level. So those children for whom school work is easy don't get bored. And those who struggle get extra help."

—Virginia Bender
Former School Board Member and Board President
Chugach School District

Standards-Based Design

Standards-based design is the nuts and bolts of the RISC Approach to Schooling. Quite simply, standards-based design means that the basic elements of schooling—what students will be taught, how that content will be taught and assessed, and how student progress will be reported—are designed and organized around standards. How these elements of schooling are addressed and integrated is what sets the RISC approach apart most dramatically, day to day, from the traditional approach to schooling. The other aspects of the RISC approach—shared vision, leadership, and continuous improvement—are the cultural dynamics that make the core standards-based elements work. Each of these is discussed in depth later in this chapter.

The RISC Approach to Standards

Standards in a RISC System

1. Standards are at the heart of the educational process.

2. Standards are *local* standards reflecting stakeholders' shared vision.

3. Developmental levels, or performance levels, are articulated in each standards area, kindergarten through high school graduation—and beyond.

4. The academic and nonacademic content specified at each level, along with the resources needed to facilitate students' progress through the levels to high school graduation, are in effect the RISC curriculum.

Standards are a well-accepted concept in education. They are what John Kendall (2003), a widely recognized expert in the development and improvement of standards for education, calls "an established fact of the American educational landscape for K–12 education" (p. 63). Simply put, standards define what students are expected to know and do at various points in their education.

Given the impact of the standards movement and the No Child Left Behind Act, educators in most schools and districts are aware of state standards in core academic areas and, at a minimum, use them as a reference to prepare students for high-stakes testing. In addition, some schools and districts have locally developed standards, but the extent to which these standards are used meaningfully—to inform decisions about instruction, classroom assessment, grading approaches, and reporting—is weak.

In a RISC school or district, standards are local standards developed based on stakeholders' shared agreement about what students should know and be able to do at each level and before they graduate from high school. Standards are articulated in core academic areas and in cross-disciplinary areas. The standards areas identified in a RISC system may include the following:

- Reading

- Writing

- Mathematics

- Science

- Social studies

- Technology literacy

- Personal, social, service

- Life skills

- The arts

- Cultural awareness and expression

- Employability

- Career development

Within each standards area, developmental levels (sometimes called performance levels or benchmarks) are created, based on what is known about how children develop, learn, and demonstrate their learning at various age levels. Figure 3.3 (pages 71 and 72) shows the performance levels developed by Highland Tech High for the Process strand of the school's Social Environments standards area. These processes are taught with the content areas of world history, geography, international and Alaska history, and United States history.

Figure 3.3: Highland Tech High. Social Environments, Processes, Levels 1–6

Level 1	
Inquisitive Thought and Creativity	Develops questions to focus inquiry and analysis
Information Processing Tools	Summarizes information through restatement
Logic and Reasoning Systems	Explores the differences between primary and secondary sources
Understanding Variability and Point of View	Identifies and describes opposing viewpoints
Mastering Action	Forms opinions based on examination of evidence
Level 2	
Inquisitive Thought and Creativity	Identifies different types of factors in a causal chain (economic, social, cultural, political, and so on)
Information Processing Tools	Forms a simple organization of main and subordinate ideas on a topic
Logic and Reasoning Systems	Develops inferences from primary and secondary sources
Understanding Variability and Point of View	Develops strategies for analyzing opposing viewpoints
Mastering Action	Forms, expresses, and explains personal points of view on issues
Level 3	
Inquisitive Thought and Creativity	Identifies and describes times when alternative courses of action would have changed the outcome of events
Information Processing Tools	States relationships between categories of information
Logic and Reasoning Systems	Develops appropriate criteria for comparing and contrasting information
Understanding Variability and Point of View	Compares and contrasts opposing viewpoints
Mastering Action	Forms, expresses, and explains opposing points of view on issues
Level 4	
Inquisitive Thought and Creativity	Reinterprets events using alternative courses of action and shows the likely effects of subsequent events
Information Processing Tools	Uses tools of visual representation for analysis (examples: decision-making trees, flow charts, webbing)
Logic and Reasoning Systems	Employs criteria for determining the validity and soundness of primary sources
Understanding Variability and Point of View	Explains how societies' values may affect an individual's point of view and interpretation of facts
Mastering Action	Participates and reflects on the political process and makes suggestions for change

Figure 3.3: Highland Tech High. Social Environments, Processes, Levels 1–6
(continued)

Level 5	
Inquisitive Thought and Creativity	Creates a causal chain on a current event and hypothesizes future outcomes
Information Processing Tools	Summarizes and develops strategies for sampling, testing, and evaluating information
Logic and Reasoning Systems	Analyzes differing primary source accounts of the same events
Understanding Variability and Point of View	Develops strategies to determine degrees of credibility in points of view
Mastering Action	Develops a well-researched and reasoned plan of action on a contemporary issue
Level 6	
Inquisitive Thought and Creativity	Develops a creative solution to a current issue based on available information
Information Processing Tools	Analyzes the impact and credibility of information from various media outlets
Logic and Reasoning Systems	Evaluates the lasting impact of primary source documents
Understanding Variability and Point of View	Analyzes opposing viewpoints to determine a course of action
Mastering Action	Implements an action plan to influence those in power regarding a contemporary issue

Source: Highland Tech High. (n.d.-a.). *Standards and Rubrics.*
Retrieved from http://www.highlandtech.org/academics/standards_and_rubrics/index.php.

These levels are the roadmap for students to progress through school to high school graduation. Together, the broad standards areas and the more detailed statements articulated at each developmental level are the heart of the educational process in every regard.

In a RISC system, locally developed standards, and their corresponding developmental levels, are based on and aligned with:

- State standards (available in 49 of 50 states, Iowa being the only exception)

- Standards developed by professional subject-area organizations (such as the National Council of Teachers of Mathematics, the American Association for the Advancement of Science, the National Council of Teachers of English, and the National Center for History in the Schools) and/or nationally recognized compendiums of standards (most notably, Mid-continent Research for Education and Learning's [McREL] *Content Knowledge: A Compendium of Content Standards for K–12 Education* [Kendall & Marzano, 2004]).

Teachers' ownership of the standards and developmental levels students must master differs in a key way from teachers' ownership of content in most schools and districts. Across the United States, individual teachers for the most part are focused only on what they must teach students at specific grade levels. In a RISC system, due to the fundamentally distinct orientation around students progressing at their own pace, individual teachers are clear about the content required for *all* of the developmental levels in all standards areas. A middle school RISC teacher with students who are tackling content in Levels 3 and 4, for example, considers all of the content students learned prior to Level 3 and all of the content students must master after Level 4. Every teacher at every grade level knows, understands, and owns the standards, developmental levels, and assessments, kindergarten through grade 12—in other words, for students' *entire educational careers*, K–12, as well as any advanced post-high school development levels articulated in particular content areas.

In fact, because RISC districts also identify advanced developmental levels for some content areas, RISC students may tackle content well beyond the high school level, at any age, K–12. Again, the reason is obvious: In a RISC school system, students are encouraged to learn and grow with no limit.

Redefining "Curriculum"

When most educators hear the word *curriculum*, they think of binders filled with lessons, some guidance about what students should learn and when they should learn it, and lists of textbooks for different subject areas that presumably, though rarely, follow the binders. Given the high-stakes environment created by the No Child Left Behind Act, many districts have spent considerable time and resources aligning their curricula with state-mandated tests. However, many of these same districts may have put little thought into whether their curriculum materials in fact align with the curriculum itself.

In a RISC school or district, curriculum is defined and approached quite differently. In a RISC system, the curriculum encompasses the content specified in the standards developmental levels identified as important by stakeholders as well as the resources teachers need to ensure that students successfully learn all of the content required at each level. In essence, in a RISC system, the standards and developmental levels *are the scope and sequence*, serving as a roadmap for student progress and ultimately graduation. Together, they answer the questions:

- What is the scope of the content that students must learn in each standards area?

- How is this content scaffolded or sequenced?

The RISC Approach to Instruction

Instruction in a RISC System

1. The mantra for instruction in a RISC environment is, "It's not about us, as teachers or administrators. It's about students." Students—their learning needs, their goals, their interests, and their unique learning styles—are put first.

2. Like the RISC approach to assessment, grading, and reporting, instruction in a RISC classroom flows from standards and is aligned with them.

3. Teachers are constantly gathering and analyzing data about student learning and using this feedback to continually make the learning environment more effective.

4. Two-way individualized *learning,* rather than one-way uniform *instruction,* is the focus.

5. Teachers move from being keepers of knowledge to facilitators of learning, and students move from being dependent to independent learners, an evolutionary process that begins as early as kindergarten.

6. The RISC Comprehensive Instructional Model includes direct instruction, but emphasizes real-world simulation and application.

This model, or a variation of it, is a common instructional model adopted and used by all teachers.

7. Thematic instruction is a primary instructional approach for making real-world connections and engaging students across ages and developmental levels.

In most schools and districts, schooling is driven by textbooks and by external, high-stakes assessments. In essence, teachers use district-approved textbooks and "wing it" from day to day, teaching what they want to teach. Conversely, in a RISC system, standards drive every aspect of the educational process, including instruction. Teachers may use textbooks but they also use a plethora of other standards-based resources.

The distinctive difference of the RISC approach to instruction can be summed up by the statement, "It's not about us. It's about kids." In a RISC system, students—what they must learn, how they are progressing, and how to make learning engaging for each student—are the highest priority. No longer is it sufficient for teachers to pull out the "September lesson file" and move through the year on the same well-worn tracks or to say, "My favorite thing to teach is literature. Let's schedule a literature class and put students in it." Teachers in RISC schools make sure they are doing things based on what students need, as dictated by students' progress in meeting standards, rather than simply teaching what they want or like to teach, or doing things "the way they have always been done."

Every aspect of every teacher's classroom learning environment, then, is oriented around what is best for students, what will help them learn, and making sure students leave each class or course that much closer to mastering the knowledge and skills they need to graduate. With that orientation in mind, all of the distinguishing characteristics that set the RISC learning experience apart from the traditional classroom setting are clear. In the RISC model, students are at the core of the instructional system, and teachers have a shared foundation to stand upon—albeit a foundation surrounded by plenty of breathing room in which to innovate. Stated differently, all of the unique dynamics of a RISC student-oriented learning environment flow naturally from a commitment to put students first.

Changing Teacher Roles: From Keepers of Knowledge to Facilitators of Learning

With Jo Clem, Board Member,
Re-Inventing Schools Coalition

So many teachers are comfortable delivering information. They view themselves as the keepers of the keys. But our job as educators is to facilitate learning, which derives from the French *facile* or from the Latin *facilis,* "easy to do." Our job is to make it easy for students to internalize whatever information we are trying to impart to them—to make it personal, and to take that knowledge and use it to make their lives richer.

I taught Shakespeare for years. For most of those years, I thought I was the keeper of the knowledge and that my job was to impart this to those who did not know. But the truth is, especially at the high school level, students already come to us knowing a lot.

When I learned this, I realized that my job wasn't about delivering information about Shakespeare's plays. It was about presenting concepts to students and then allowing them to process these concepts—to see, for example, whether personality characteristics had changed from the time Shakespeare wrote his plays to the current time.

When I realized that I could teach *Romeo and Juliet* in this way, it was amazing what students began to see about life, about themselves, about human beings, about love. I would say to students, "Let's see how these people are like us or not. And if they are, what can we learn from Shakespeare about joy and sorrow and the depth of feelings? What does *Romeo and Juliet* say about us? Would you climb a ladder to get to the one you love? Would you risk your friends making fun of you to spend time with someone they don't like?" One student said to me, "You know, *Romeo and Juliet* is really about parents being so stupid that they get in the way of their children really knowing what love is all about." My job was to open the window for students. My job—our job as educators—is to build bridges between what students currently know and what they need to know—and then get out of the way.

The RISC environment can be more specifically described as a standards-based, student-directed, individualized, and data-based learning environment emphasizing increasingly real-life application. Like all of the elements of the RISC Approach to Schooling, the context for instruction and learning is a dedication to continuous improvement toward excellence in professional practice and every student reaching the highest possible levels of achievement.

A Standards- and Data-Based Environment

Given the increasingly widespread acceptance of standards as a necessary element of education, lists of standards can be found posted on the walls of most U.S. classrooms. At the beginning of each school year, many teachers also announce the standards that will be covered that year. But the simple adoption of standards means very little in terms of student learning. The instructional process must flow from and be aligned with standards, and there must be processes in place to ensure that this is occurring. If lesson planning and day-to-day instruction occur independent of standards, then standards are relatively meaningless statements.

To combat this lack of alignment between standards and learning, administrators in RISC schools regularly observe classrooms, teachers monitor themselves, and teachers observe and give feedback to their colleagues. The perspective of administrators and teachers is, "We're in this together for the benefit of students."

The integrity of the link between standards and learning also is maintained by the ongoing use of data. Teachers continually strengthen the learning environment based on data collected from a range of sources, including the following:

- Classroom assessment in its many forms—tests, assignments, presentations, projects, oral reports, student interviews, and formal and informal conversations with students

- District-level assessments

- State-mandated exams

Educators use information and statistics from these sources to make needed adjustments in classroom practice. As discussed further in the next section of this chapter (The RISC Approach to Assessment, on page 88), frequent classroom assessment results in many data points about student progress in mastering specific content; this feedback is used to continually shape instruction, address gaps in students' understanding or skill, and accelerate student achievement. In addition to scores and information from assessments, RISC administrators and teachers also monitor *leading indicators* of student achievement by asking questions about engagement and motivation, for example: Are students more engaged in learning? Are students motivated and interested?

Student-Directed Individualized Learning

For years, leading educators, researchers, and writers have argued that the educational process must shift from a focus on teachers to a focus on students and learning. As Larry Lezotte put it in a 2002 interview, "What we need to do is transform the system from a teacher-centered system to a learning-centered system" (Sellers, 2002).

This idea is relatively common knowledge; the problem is that it is not common practice. In most schools across the United States, the instructional process is one way; teachers deliver knowledge to students, who absorb it or not. Conversely, a distinctive feature of a RISC environment is that *two-way individualized learning,* rather than *one-way uniform instruction,* is the focus. Learning is a dynamic process of students talking about, thinking about, analyzing, applying, and otherwise interacting with concepts, themes, facts, and skills they are learning. Student learning, facilitated by teachers and over time directed by students themselves, is individualized to students' needs, and every strategy possible is used to ensure that learning is maximized.

In a RISC system, students *themselves* are encouraged, taught, and empowered to be accountable for their learning. This is not a black-and-white, step-by-step, to-do list through which students become leaders of the learning process overnight. Rather, it is an evolutionary process in which students move from being dependent to independent learners. In a

RISC system, teachers are accountable for student learning; in fact, students hold them accountable. Once students own the system and understand the direction they are headed in their education, they become advocates who begin to insist that teachers help them accomplish their goals. But students, too, become accountable for their own learning. Rather than simply sitting back and absorbing knowledge from lectures and assignments, they begin to design and lead their own learning process.

Teaching and empowering students to be leaders of their own education begins as early as kindergarten. Teachers show their young students the standards they need to learn, teach them how to set goals, and begin to tie students' interests to whatever standards they are learning, whether in reading, writing, teamwork, or using technology. As students mature, teachers continually assess students' readiness to take more leadership of their learning and over time turn over more and more leadership of the learning process to students. Eventually, students lead conversations and conferences with their teachers; they choose the specific standards they will incorporate into their next project; and they set specific goals about what they will learn and by when. In short, students not only have a say in how their education goes—they are in very real ways at the helm.

By the time students are in upper elementary school, teachers still are accountable for students' learning, but their role is more that of a facilitator or mentor. This change requires a shift in mindset, even for RISC teachers. Similarly and more dramatically, teachers who move from a more traditional setting to a RISC system must make that shift in mindset as they take on very different roles. As they make that shift, the types of tasks they spend time on change, as shown in Figure 3.4 on page 80.

Figure 3.4: Teacher Roles—Traditional Classroom Versus RISC Classroom

Traditional Classroom	RISC Classroom
Teachers spend more of their time . . .	Teachers spend more of their time . . .
• Lecturing	• Engaging students
• Managing classroom behavior	• Empowering, mentoring, guiding, and inspiring students to take control of their learning
• Scoring papers and tests	
• Preparing bulletin boards	• Coaching students about how to move forward
• Updating grade books	
• Preparing for state testing	• Assessing students' ability levels
	• Providing individualized small- and large-group instruction
	• Creating effective and engaging ways in which to increase individual student achievement
	• Communicating what *proficient* and *advanced* work look like

In one sense, teaching in a RISC setting requires more time in terms of tracking students' progress (see discussion in Grading and Reporting section, which follows on page 94). In another sense, RISC teachers find themselves more at ease as teachers, as Highland Tech High Assistant Principal Rebecca Midles explains:

> It doesn't matter what age students are. Once they grasp the [RISC] model, people don't understand this, but my job is easier. As a teacher, I have more time to listen and learn from the students and be more at an observational level. Once students own the model, when they tell you what they need and they show you what they are learning, when you see the light bulb go off—when you get into that phase of students getting *inside* their learning— when that happens, they are the authors of their future.

Students have a tremendous opportunity to take the reins from teachers and to learn, progress at their own pace, and, if they wish, graduate early—with more knowledge and skill under their belts than the average student of the past. A pitfall for RISC teachers is passively sitting back and letting students educate themselves, which can result in students falling behind. This is a significant and potentially costly misunderstanding of the RISC approach. An ongoing focus for district leaders must be to continually educate teachers about their role in the new system and help them understand that they must continue to be actively engaged in the learning process—supporting students, encouraging and guiding them, and pulling those who are sinking back up to the surface.

The idea that students are leaders of the learning process goes hand in hand with the individualization of the learning experience. Although some schools across the country are in the preliminary stages of aligning their classroom practices with academic standards, all students in age-based grade levels generally receive the same instruction, delivered in the same way, rather than instruction individualized to students' varying learning styles and their level of understanding of the content they are learning.

Conversely, every student in a RISC school has a Personal Learning Plan, which emphasizes real-life application and details how students will progress through the developmental levels at their own pace. A middle school student's Personal Learning Plan may include, for instance, a goal to master the graduation-level content for all of his district's core academic standards—reading, writing, math, science, and social studies—by his first year in high school. His plan also might include shorter term goals and structures for fulfillment such as a schedule of completion dates for projects demonstrating his mastery of interim developmental levels as well as assessments to make sure he is on track to meet his goals.

Beyond Direct Instruction

In RISC schools and districts, direct instruction is still alive and well, for instance when an entire classroom or a smaller group of students are learning the same content at the same time. However, generally speaking, opportunities for students to apply what they are learning dominate classroom time.

The broad types of strategies RISC teachers use are captured in the RISC Comprehensive Instructional Model, summarized in Figure 3.5 (page 82). This model is an integrated set of strategies, emphasizing real-world simulation and application, that is designed to actively and continually engage students using the best teaching practices. This model, or a variation of it, is used in RISC schools and districts—not because it is mandated, but because staff members discuss their approach to teaching and learning and come to an agreement about the model they all will use. As noted earlier in this chapter, a shared philosophy about instruction is one of the tight aspects of a RISC system. Everyone is on the same page about instruction, drawing on a shared repertoire of classroom strategies and sharing insights as well as materials and instructional resources. The result is a synergy of learning and growth, both for teachers and students.

Figure 3.5: The RISC Comprehensive Instructional Model

Direct Instruction
Traditional teaching emphasizes lecture and teacher presentation.
Application of Skills
Students apply knowledge and practice skills.
Classroom Application. Students apply knowledge and practice skills in different contexts.
Interactive Simulation. Students apply knowledge and practice skills through role-playing or simulations.
Real-Life Connection. Students apply knowledge and practice skills in meaningful real-life situations.

The RISC Comprehensive Instructional Model is based on the principle that students are more deeply engaged and empowered in learning—and therefore the complexity of the learning process grows—as instruction moves from being teacher centered to student centered; in other words, instruction changes as students move up the scale from listening to a lecture to teaching others. In addition, as students move from classroom application to simulation to real-life connections, their ownership and independence in applying their growing knowledge increases, while teacher support and guidance decreases.

The purposes of using a variety of instructional approaches are to:

- Help students make meaningful connections between the world and the knowledge and skills they are learning.

- Engage and inspire students, while preventing apathy.

- Use the learning strategies that are most appropriate for the knowledge or skills students are learning.

- Deepen and extend students' learning by enhancing their ability to apply knowledge and skills in new and unpredictable situations.

- Reach every student, given his or her unique learning style.

> "In a RISC system, everyone knows what the instructional targets are and everyone works together to do whatever it takes to get every child to those instructional targets. If it takes a little more time for a particular student, it takes a little more time. If it takes a little bit different strategy for another student, then we do that.
>
> "We give extra and external opportunities to any student who is capable of taking advantage of those. We certainly don't insist that students sit in our classrooms if we can find additional opportunities—whether in our district or outside it—to help extend their learning."
>
> —Greg Johnson
> Director of Curriculum and Instruction
> Bering Strait School District

Thematic Units and Real-World Experiences

One of the core ways in which the heights of learning are realized in a RISC setting is through the use of thematic units that can be extended and applied to real-world settings. A thematic unit integrates academic and nonacademic standards—core subject areas as well as cross-disciplinary strands (so-called 21st-century skills)—under the umbrella of a broad idea (such as leadership, democracy, the nature of communities, or human conflict) or an integrated system (such as a city, animal habitats, or an ecosystem). Thematic instruction is a hallmark of a RISC learning environment in at least two ways: its emphasis on real-world learning and its usefulness as a cross-age, cross-grade-level approach.

A thematic unit pulls together state, district, and/or local standards into a coherent whole that reflects the real-life ways in which human beings seamlessly (and, for the most part, unconsciously) draw on everything they learned in school and in life. Whether you are shopping for groceries at your local supermarket, determining what is wrong with your car and figuring out how to get it repaired, seeking approval from the city for a neighborhood street barbeque, or planning a month-long trip to Tibet—you are "pulling it all together" from a mental databank.

A strong RISC thematic unit engages students in the classroom, but also takes them outside the walls of the schools into nature, into the community, and into local businesses—in short, into the real world. What better way to prepare students for life than to engage them in life?

Students who want to work in an urban environment, for instance, but who live in rural America and have limited access to urban areas, need opportunities to visit and perhaps work in urban areas. Conversely, a student in downtown Chicago who wants to be a farmer needs opportunities to spend time on a farm, to experience firsthand what it means to be a farmer on a day-to-day basis. These real-world experiences help students make better choices about life paths and expand their view of what is possible for them. At a very simplistic level, it is easy to see that simply understanding a concept or knowing about a career makes little difference. Even lots and lots of information about a career is a far cry from actually doing the job. In essence, in a RISC system, students are educated anywhere, any place, any time.

The second way in which thematic units resonate with the RISC philosophy is that they can easily be used with students of differing ages and ability levels. All students in a class—or even a group of classes—can work on the same theme, but students can work on specific standards at their own particular developmental level. Individual instruction, small- and large-group instruction, and application activities vary depending on the developmental levels that individual students have mastered and those they are working on during the unit.

"Many people ask questions about how it works when students are working on different levels. I really didn't look at the differences in levels or ages of students. It never really occurred to me. It was just the difference in the work I was doing. Some 8th graders may be working on level 4 in math, while some 10th graders may be level 2, and sometimes they are in the same class. A lot of people wonder whether that works. Actually, the diversity benefits everyone. Students and teachers work well together and interact in all kinds of ways. For example, higher level students help students who are working at lower levels, which doesn't just help the lower level students, but the higher level students, too. It's one thing to understand it. It's another thing to teach it. So it's taking another step in the learning process."

—Zach Maurer, Graduate
Highland Tech High,
Anchorage, Alaska

Planning an effective, well-integrated thematic unit takes time and thoughtful reflection. Figure 3.6 (pages 86 and 87) illustrates how a teacher in a RISC system might plan a multi-age unit around the theme of working in a city for students who are learning standards ranging across developmental levels that roughly align with grades 4 through 8. Students apply what they are learning through roles they take on in the city. As the unit unfolds, students might come together, for a morning or for a full day, for instance, to have the experience of working and living together in a city.

Students in RISC multi-level, multi-age learning environments work at a variety of levels in different content areas. Assume, for instance, that Matt is operating at level 8 in mathematics, but level 4 in all other standards areas. He uses his level 4 writing and reading skills to write an application to become an architect, read level 4 books about architecture as a career, and write about the skills he needs to master the field. As an architect contracted by the city, he must prepare goals to present to the mayor.

Figure 3.6: Planning a Multi-Age Thematic Activity, Levels 4–8

Standards Areas

Career Development (CD), Reading (R), Writing (W), Mathematics (M)

Discussion Questions

Direct Instruction

Application, Simulation, and Real-Life Connection Activities

Theme: Working in a City

Sample Standards

(CD) Level 4. Employs skills to be a team player (for example, cooperation, acceptance of roles, sportsmanship)

(CD) Level 6. Demonstrates flexibility, adaptability, and resiliency while maintaining a positive attitude (through perseverance, acceptance, problem-solving, and patience)

(R) Level 5. Expresses own opinion about material read, and supports opinions with textual evidence

(R) Level 7. Reads and applies multi-step directions to perform complex procedures and tasks

(W) Level 4. Writes paragraphs that stay on topic and includes details to support the main idea

(W) Level 6. Writes using appropriate voice for audience

(M) Level 4. Adds and subtracts three-digit whole numbers

(M) Level 8. Uses proportions to solve problems involving scale drawings, area, and perimeter

Sample Discussion Questions

(CD) Think about a time that you were part of a team (such as a soccer team, a Cub Scouts or Girl Scouts team, or any time you worked together with friends or others). Who were the best team players? What made them the best?

(R) What are the different types of materials you might read in the workplace? (Offer examples, if needed, to prompt students' thinking, such as charts, graphs, books, online articles, and directions on a piece of equipment.) What kinds of skills might you need to understand what you read?

(W) What are the components of a well-written piece?

(M) What are the math skills needed for various city roles, such as an assessor, an architect, and a bank teller?

Figure 3.6: Planning a Multi-Age Thematic Activity, Levels 4–8 *(continued)*

Sample Direct Instruction

(CD) Define the characteristics of an effective team player. Explain organizational hierarchies and chains of command.

(R) Distinguish the characteristics of different types of text and the elements of text, such as author's voice, main ideas, literary devices, and supporting points.

(W) Prepare lessons on voice, prewriting strategies, structure, punctuation, revising and editing, and theme.

(M) Prepare lessons on basic math facts, computation and problem-solving strategies, as well as principles of algebra and geometry, with those students who are ready for this level of content.

Sample Application, Simulation, and Real-Life Connections

Students complete sample resumes and job applications, and practice interviewing and customer-service skills. Students have the option to participate in on-site job shadowing opportunities through community businesses.

Students read a variety of resources for background information about their city role.

Students take on city jobs and track their success. Each student has a classroom checkbook. Students earn money from jobs, rent homes they own, pay taxes, and buy property.

Students work in teams to tackle an identified city issue, such as writing a proposal to the city government to secure more funding for the fire department.

Students create job descriptions and performance goals for their positions in the classroom city. Periodically throughout the unit, students write a self-evaluation of how well they are performing their city role.

Matt's math skills prepare him to do the actual work of an architect: designing homes for other students in the classroom city. Once he has established his reputation in the city and has mastered the skills needed to design residential buildings, he then moves on to designing more complex buildings such as hospitals. The mathematics skills he needs for this career are advanced. He must understand, for instance, how to accurately portray proportion, surface area, and perimeter in his architectural drawings.

Amy, a judge for the classroom city, draws on different skills from different developmental levels. Her mathematics skills are level 4; her interpersonal skills, level 6. As a city judge, Amy must be fair, equitable, and adaptable, yet resilient. She creates the process for court proceedings, helps resolve conflicts, and oversees the process of the class developing a code of ethics for how the city will operate.

The enormous value of classroom simulations such as this lies in the distinction between understanding a concept—even in great depth—and putting it into practice. The Harry Potter movie *The Order of the Phoenix* includes an enjoyable, vivid example of this difference. A new teacher, Dolores Umbridge, forbids her students from practicing any actual magic, while using dry, rote practices such as having students write something four times since, she says, this will ensure that they have memorized it. While Professor Umbridge lords over her students, Harry, as teacher, and two dozen of his fellow students find a secret room at Hogwarts where they practice day after day and, over time, begin to truly master their skills. This is a fun, clear example of the fact that it is one thing to grasp a distinction at the conceptual level; it is quite another to apply it in real-life settings.

The RISC Approach to Assessment

Assessment in a RISC System

1. RISC educators administer frequent, formative district and classroom assessments that are used to make microadjustments in teaching and learning.

2. The power of classroom assessment is tapped through a wide range of formal and informal ways of gathering information about students' developing knowledge and skill—from traditional tests, essays, and oral responses to student interviews and peer assessments.

3. Common, internally developed assessments are used by all teachers.

4. Testing is approached collaboratively. *Prior to testing*, students know the type of assessment that will be used and are clear about the criteria that will be used to judge their performance.

5. Over time, students begin to help design their own assessments.

The accurate and timely assessment of students' progress is a vital element of any educational environment. As such, like the other elements of standards-based design—in fact, all the aspects of the RISC Approach to

Schooling—a RISC school or district's assessment program is continually revisited to ensure that it is based on research and best practice. This section highlights a few of the key differences between RISC's assessment practices and those long in use in U.S. schools.

The Power of Classroom Assessment

A RISC system differs from the long-standing, traditional approach to assessment in the emphasis placed on classroom assessment. This emphasis is consistent with Marzano's (2006) findings that classroom assessment can have a dramatic effect on student achievement:

> To the surprise of some educators, major reviews of the research on the effects of classroom assessment indicate that it might be one of the most powerful weapons in a teacher's arsenal. (p. 2)

All schools in the United States must administer state-mandated tests to students at the end of specific grades or during specific grade-level bands.* RISC schools and districts are no exception. Even those Alaska school systems that have received a waiver from the state Carnegie unit graduation requirement must administer assessments to students in the required subjects at the required age/grade levels. However, RISC leaders recognize that although the data available from these assessments provide some useful information about trends in overall student performance, for a number of reasons—the infrequency of testing, the lag in availability of test results, and the summing of students' test item responses to a single proficiency score—state tests as currently designed do not provide the kind of information needed to improve the teaching and learning environment (see Stiggins, 2005).

Conversely, more frequent district assessments, particularly classroom assessments, provide feedback that can be used formatively and effectively to make microadjustments in teaching and learning—and therefore accelerate student learning. Using assessments in this way means that instruction and assessment are partnered in a continuous cycle of establishing

---

*The No Child Left Behind Act requires states to administer assessments in math and reading or language arts in each of grades 3–8 and at least once during grades 10–12. States also must administer science assessments at least once during grades 3–5, grades 6–9, and grades 10–12, a requirement that went into effect with the 2007–2008 academic year. See U.S. Department of Education, 2002.

individual student learning goals, measuring and celebrating progress, making adjustments, and setting new learning goals.

Multiple Types of Assessment

One of the most valuable aspects of the RISC approach to assessment is the use of a variety of classroom assessments to measure students' levels of understanding and skill. In spite of what we have learned about the value of using an array of classroom assessment types, many teachers continue to rely primarily on textbooks' end-of-chapter quizzes and tests to measure students' progress in specific courses. In RISC schools, on the other hand, teachers gather many data points about students' levels of knowledge and skill. In essence, they draw on a repertoire of assessments, including the following traditional approaches as well as other modes not traditionally viewed as assessments:

- Essays

- Oral responses and reports

- Projects

- Portfolios

- Observations of students as they work

- Interviews and meetings with students

- Student self-assessments

- Peer assessments

- Forced choice, true/false, and short answer, multiple choice

Multiple assessment tools are used for at least two reasons. First, students learn in different ways. For instance, one student may learn best by reading information, and another by listening to a teacher or peer explain a concept or principle. Just as students learn in different ways, the ways in which they best demonstrate their learning can vary.

While the learning process in a RISC setting may sometimes be traditional in that new content may be presented directly, it is the student's choice how he or she will demonstrate that he or she really knows that content. Indeed, there is a plethora of ways for students to demonstrate that concepts are within their grasp, and all can be equally valid—whether a student draws a picture, writes a song, takes a written or verbal test, creates a class presentation, or puts together a collage.

The second reason that multiple assessments are used in RISC settings is that different types of assessments are appropriate for different types of knowledge and skill (see Marzano, 2006, pp. 59–88, specifically the top of p. 76). For example, students' recalling of facts and details might be best assessed through short answer or multiple choice questions, whereas students' abilities to apply knowledge or use skills is better assessed through projects or presentations.

RISC assessments fall into four primary categories:

- **Traditional assessments**—Assessments of a student's knowledge through basic recall of facts and details using multiple choice, true/false, open-ended responses, short answer, and other traditional assessments

- **Analytical assessments**—Assessments of a student's ability to apply the knowledge and skills they are learning

- **Contextual assessments**—Assessments of the quality of a student's performance and his or her application of skills in the context of a real-world situation

- **Student self-assessments**—Self-assessments of knowledge and skills related to a particular standards developmental level

In addition to using these four broad types of assessment, two additional points should be highlighted here, again drawing on Marzano's work. These deal with the frequency of assessment and the type of feedback provided to students. In both instances, research is our guide.

Frequency and Feedback

"One of the strongest findings from the research," Marzano reports, "is that the frequency of assessments is related to student academic achievement" (2006, p. 9). Generally speaking, the more often teachers take stock of students' relative strengths and weaknesses and use this information to guide instruction, the greater the gains in student achievement (see Marzano, 2006, pp. 9–10).

Relative to student feedback, findings from research might best be summed up by saying that feedback in and of itself is not necessarily useful. In fact, the long-used practice of simply telling students which answers are right and which are wrong (a practice with which most readers likely have considerable firsthand experience) has a negative influence on student learning (see Bangert-Drowns, Kulik, Kulik, & Morgan [1991], cited in Marzano, 2006). Conversely, ensuring that students are clear about the criteria that will be used to judge their responses, providing students with the correct answers, giving them explanations about why their responses were correct or incorrect, and asking students to continue responding to an assessment item until they correctly answer are all practices that research shows can result in statistically significant gains in student achievement (Marzano, 2006).

Student Ownership and Teacher Collaboration

Another point about assessment in a RISC system that is alluded to in these examples of useful feedback is students' ownership of and involvement in the assessment process. A fundamental principle of the RISC Approach to Schooling is that student motivation and engagement have a great deal to do with student success. Therefore, in a RISC system, learning is not the result of winning a guessing game. Teachers make sure students know what they need to learn at each level, the kind of assessments that will be used, how they will be graded, and how their grades will be reported.

Testing—often viewed as something to keep highly secret from students—is approached collaboratively in a RISC system. Students know the type of assessment that will be used in advance; it is not a mystery to them how their knowledge and skill will be tested. Teachers provide scoring guides and administer practice exams in the same format as the actual assessment. In fact, when the RISC approach is deployed at a high level, teachers teach students about the process to the point where students begin to help design the assessments themselves. This is an evolutionary process that sets a RISC system apart from other education systems.

This approach to assessment is consistent with what assessment expert Rick Stiggins (2005) calls "assessment FOR learning" (p. 327). Stiggins makes a distinction between our long-standing view of formative assessment as something that provides *teachers* with information about students, and formative assessment *for* learning, which provides a "continuing stream of evidence" about student achievement to teachers *as well as* parents and students (p. 327). As explained by Stiggins, the most important difference between these two approaches to formative assessment is student involvement:

> Students play a special role in communicating evidence of learning to one another, to their teacher, and to their families, and they do so not just after the learning has been completed but all along the journey to success. In short, during the learning, students are inside the assessment process, watching themselves grow, feeling in control of their success, and believing that continued success is within reach if they keep trying. . . . Assessment FOR learning rests on the understanding that students are data-based instructional decision makers too. (pp. 327–328)

Further, citing findings from research, Stiggins (2005, p. 328) notes that when student-centered assessment practices are approached consistently and routinely, substantial achievement gains—as much as one-half to two standard deviations on high-stakes tests—can result, particularly for low achievers.

In addition to using a range of classroom assessment types, educators in RISC schools are continually challenged to systematically and thoughtfully administer classroom tests, provide student feedback in ways that best encourage learning, and show students how to take more leadership of their own education. The phrase "continually challenged" is used deliberately here to emphasize the point that a RISC system is, by definition, a constantly improving system striving for excellence. RISC teachers and others who choose to pursue continuous improvement are never at an endpoint in their development as educators; they are always looking to research and best practice for strategies to enhance student achievement.

This commitment to excellence is partly realized by the atmosphere of collaboration and shared learning that is a hallmark of a RISC environment.

In a traditional school, an individual teacher may have discovered an effective way to measure student progress, but because a systematic (and systemic) approach to assessment is lacking, a teacher down the hall may miss out on this important learning.

Conversely, in a RISC system, there is a systemic approach to assessment, *common* internal assessments are used by all teachers, and there is a shared, ongoing conversation for improving assessment. When staff have a common vocabulary and common measurement tools, communication and collaboration are enhanced, better decisions can be made about students, and the school or district is in a stronger position relative to its accountability to meet not only the letter of federal and state mandates, but the spirit of ensuring that every child has the best chance of achieving his or her potential.

The RISC Approach to Grading and Reporting

Grading and Reporting in a RISC System

1. Consistent, shared grading processes minimize grading inconsistencies among teachers and increase grading validity and reliability.

2. Students' progress in meeting individual standards is assessed using a four-point rubric, most notably: emerging, developing, proficient, and advanced.

3. Students move to the next developmental level when they have demonstrated proficient or better performance—the equivalent of at least a B—on standards-based assessments. For this reason, RISC's grading approach can be described as "A, B, or Try Again."

4. Student progress toward mastering the developmental levels is documented and reported through detailed standards-based report cards.

5. RISC report cards help teachers, parents, and students track the standards levels students are focusing on, as well as students' depth of knowledge, facility with required skills, and the quality of work within those levels.

6. Because of the differences between a traditional approach to education and the RISC Approach to Schooling, schools and districts

implementing the RISC approach are encouraged to use the term *recording* instead of *grading* to help educators and other stakeholders shift their mindset from traditional notions of grading.

RISC report cards help teachers, parents, and students track the standards levels students are focusing on, as well as students' depth of knowledge, facility with required skills, and the quality of work within those levels.

Grading Versus *Recording*

Like other aspects of the RISC Approach to Schooling, grading is viewed quite differently in a RISC setting compared to the long-standing grading system in use in most schools in the United States. In addition, consistent with their dedication to continuous improvement, RISC staff members, as well as leaders of RISC schools and districts, are committed to continually strengthening RISC's grading processes by drawing on the best research-based guidance available. This section touches on a few of the distinctive aspects of RISC's standards-based grading practices relative to assessments of students' progress.

In a traditional A–F grading system, it is a long-used practice to give students a single grade—whether on a specific assignment, test, project, or presentation. The potential disadvantages of such an orientation are multiple and have been studied extensively by education researchers (for example, Marzano, 2000, 2006; Marzano & Kendall, 1996; Stiggins, 2005; Stiggins, Arter, Chappuis, & Chappuis, 2005).

Learning rarely covers a narrow band of knowledge or skill. Thematic units, in particular, cover a number of content areas. A unit on ecosystems, for example, may draw on a student's understanding of systems in nature, his or her skill in applying the scientific process, and the student's writing skill in explaining findings. In addition to content knowledge and skill, many teachers—consciously or unconsciously—consider a student's attitude, class participation, timeliness in turning in assignments, and other nonacademic, often value-based measures as they assign a single grade. As a result, when a student receives a single letter grade, typically it is unclear how much of the grade is reflective of the student's academic performance on varying topics or standards and how much is reflective of nonacademic, though valid, dimensions (sometimes called life skills).

Further, what an A means in one class is often quite different from what an A means in a different class; this variation occurs even among classes focused on the same content area and delivered at the same grade level. Each individual teacher is likely to have a different perspective about what constitutes acceptable or exemplary work. In addition, typically there is great variance among the criteria teachers consider when giving an A, a B, and so on, and how much weight they assign to each criterion. To further muddy the grading waters, teachers frequently change their grading criteria from year to year. In other words, in a traditional education system, there can be a great deal of subjectivity and inconsistency about grading.

These issues can arise in a RISC system, but they are less likely to occur when consistent, shared grading processes are followed relative to judgments about students' performance. A hallmark of staff collaboration in RISC systems is frequent discussion and work sessions. For example, teachers work together to determine what constitutes a "proficient" paper and which benchmark papers will be used to gauge students' writing skills. Because these types of conversations and processes take place schoolwide, grading approaches in a RISC school are more valid, reliable, and authentic than they are in a non-standards-based school—*regardless* of which teacher is doing the grading.

There are a number of ways in which a RISC school might choose to assess students' progress in meeting individual standards. Many RISC schools use a four-point rubric, as follows:

- Advanced

- Proficient

- Developing

- Emerging

As noted earlier, the use of common rubrics is one of the tight aspects of a RISC system. The advantage of a rubric over the traditional A–F grading approach is that a rubric clarifies teachers' expectations regarding student performance at various levels. Could the letter grades of A, B, C, D, or F be used instead of the descriptive phrases noted here? Of course. The advantage of a rubric is that the use of these terms is a constant reminder that challenges the A–F grading mindset. Further, the use of descriptive indicators of student proficiency, rather than an A–F scale, provides additional specificity for teachers, students, and parents. A grade of B on the other hand, although more familiar to both parents and students and therefore more welcoming, tells them relatively little about the student's mastery of the content.

How these progress levels are described and applied to students' performance depends on the type of assessment being used. Figure 3.7 shows how rubrics might be used for an analytical assessment (in this case, in reading).

Figure 3.7: Highland Tech High. Reading Level 1. Sample Rubrics

RL.ST.01.01 Applies pre-reading strategies to the text (set a purpose, focus attention, predict using title, and so on)			
Advanced	**Proficient**	**Developing**	**Emerging**
Teaches various pre-reading strategies to others	Uses two of the following pre-reading strategies: setting a purpose, focusing attention, predicting	Uses one pre-reading strategy	Attempts to apply one pre-reading strategy during reading situations
RL.ST.01.02 Makes connections from prior knowledge to the text			
Advanced	**Proficient**	**Developing**	**Emerging**
Uses multiple details or pieces of evidence to analyze the connections made	Consistently applies relevant prior knowledge to texts (self, world, or other texts)	Usually connects some prior knowledge to texts	Attempts to connect prior knowledge to texts
RL.ST.01.03 Demonstrates understanding of plot by sequencing events in chronological order from a given passage			
Advanced	**Proficient**	**Developing**	**Emerging**
Explains to others how to sequence events and/or demonstrates the ability to sequence events in a more complex text	Consistently sequences events in chronological order	Is able to sequence some events in order	Begins to recognize and sequence events

Source: Excerpted from Highland Tech High. (n.d.-a). Standards and Rubrics. See Reading and literature, Rubrics, Reading L.1. Anchorage, AK: Author. Accessed at http://www.highlandtech.org/academics/standards_and_rubrics/index.php on September 12, 2008.

The four-point rubric can be used for more traditional assessments (such as forced choice, true/false, or fill in the blank), but in these instances the rubric levels are essentially percentage scales for correctly answered test items. These scales can be roughly assigned to the RISC rubric levels, with *emerging* equating to 60–69%, *developing* equating to 70–79%, *proficient* equating to 80–89%, and *advanced* equating to 90–100%. The difference in a RISC system is that when percentage rubrics are used, they are used to make decisions about instruction, not as a gatekeeper or determinant for moving students ahead.

In addition to the use of rubrics, another key way in which the RISC approach challenges the long-standing A–F grading mindset is by encouraging schools and districts to use the term *recording* in place of the term *grading*. As students engage in various assessments of their performance, teachers (and students) assess students' mastery of required content and skills, select different rubric levels, and record notes and comments about a variety of issues that become part of a body of feedback about students' progress. At its highest and best implementation, a RISC system is a seamless, fully aligned, transparent system of students' participating in various assessments, teachers and others recording notes and comments about students' demonstrated performance on different types of assessments for different standards, and the system then reporting this wealth of information to students, parents, and other stakeholders. Because a RISC system is fully aligned, RISC districts have the ability to compare the progress of groups of students over time, to document the types of assessments on which students excel, and most notably, to conduct predictability studies on students' ability to pass state exams with 95–99% accuracy.

In a traditional education system, students move ahead to the next grade level—and presumably more challenging academic content—when they achieve a minimum score or grade, typically a D or D–. In a RISC system, students also move ahead only when they achieve a minimum score, grade, or rubric level, but in a RISC system, the bar is set much higher; students move to the next developmental level when they demonstrate a proficient or better level of understanding or skill—the equivalent of at least a B. In other words, students take on more advanced content only when it is clear that they truly know and can use the content addressed in that level. For this reason, RISC's grading approach—RISC's approach to recording information about assessments of students' growing mastery in different standards—is frequently and accurately described as "A, B, or Try Again."

Reporting

In a RISC system, student progress toward mastering the developmental levels is documented and reported through standards-based report cards. As is the case with everything else in a RISC system, the process of tracking and communicating feedback about students' progress is comprehensive and geared toward providing relevant, useful information about individual students. Figures 3.8 (pages 100–101) and 3.9 (page 102) show different approaches that two RISC districts have taken to conveying this information to parents and students. The Bering Strait School District's report card, shown in Figure 3.8, is one document of several the district uses to provide a comprehensive, detailed perspective on a student's growth over time.

As Figures 3.8 and 3.9 show, a RISC report card—what might also be called a *snapshot of student progress*—offers a far more complete picture of students' progress than a traditional, single-grade-based report card. These information-rich reports help teachers, parents, and students track not only which levels students are focusing on, but their scope and depth of knowledge, their facility with required skills, and the quality of their work within those levels.

Tracking and Monitoring Students' Progress

Efficiently and effectively tracking and analyzing students' progress on any set of standards is a challenge—and a benefit—in the RISC standards-based system. Computer software that allows teachers and administrators to electronically enter and manage students' scores relative to the content covered by each of the standards developmental levels is a virtual necessity. The Data Analysis and Reporting Toolkit (DART), is an open source software tool developed by Alaska's Bering Strait School District (see http://wiki.bssd.org/index.php/DART_System). Another useful tool is "E-ducate," developed by Three Shapes LLC (see www.3shapes.com). See chapter 4 for further discussion of the advantages of quality grading and reporting software programs.

Figure 3.8: Report Card for Unalakleet Schools, Bering Strait School District

Student Name: Susan Justice	Year/Quarter: 2008–2009/Q1
Level Progress Descriptors	Quality Performance Indicators (QPI)
(ADV) Advanced Student exceeds mastery expectations and is able to extend his or her knowledge to make new connections in this content area.	**Exemplary** Student is a self-directed learner and exceeds teacher expectations in all areas of work quality, progress toward mastery of standards, and timeliness of class work.
(PRO) Proficient Student has demonstrated mastery of all standards, has passed all district assessments, and demonstrates that he or she can apply these standards in real-world settings.	**Acceptable** Student performance met teacher expectations in the following areas: quality of work; progress toward mastery of standards; and turning in class work on time, most of the time.
(DEV) Developing Student has demonstrated mastery of some standards and is beginning to show application of new knowledge.	**Deficient** Student is attempting to make progress but has not yet met one or more of the expected outcomes for "acceptable."
(EMG) Emerging Student is beginning to acquire the knowledge necessary to demonstrate the successful mastery of standards in this level.	**Disengaged** Student is making little or no progress due to a lack of performance or participation.
	Not Instructed This content was not taught during the last quarter.

Figure 3.8: Report Card for Unalakleet Schools, Bering Strait School District *(continued)*

Level Title	Level	Overall	QPI	Comments
Cultural Awareness	CA 7	DEV	Exemplary	Susan is doing an excellent job in this level. Her work on assembling a subsistence-gathering calendar and presenting it in both English and Inupiaq was outstanding.
Career Skills	CS 5	DEV	Acceptable	She went to the Job Center and used the ALEXsys program to locate jobs. She also worked on her interview skills, participated in a job-shadowing program, and identified a potential career to pursue.
Life Skills	LS 8	EMG	Acceptable	Susan learned about social etiquette and the social parameters of an interview. The importance of being a good listener while speaking with a future employer was stressed.
Mathematics	MA 11	DEV	Acceptable	Susan has greatly improved her algebra and graphing skills this quarter.
Reading	RE 9	EMG	Exemplary	Her skills and comprehension are consistently excellent.
Science	SC 7L	DEV	Exemplary	Susan scored proficient on the end-of-learning assessment and the standards for the Ecology Strand in Life Science.
Social Studies	SS 8A	DEV	Acceptable	She did a very good job comparing and contrasting how the budget was built for the State of Alaska in 2007 versus how it was done in 1947 when Alaska was a U.S. Territory.
Technology	TE 5	DEV	Acceptable	Susan helped create the Unalakleet Schools web site and plans to maintain/update the site regularly.
Writing	WR 8	DEV	Exemplary	Her writing shows maturity, depth, and insight.

Source: Bering Strait School District, Unalakleet, Alaska.

Note: This report card, as well as a version without the Quality Performance Indicators, is available to all schools in the district. For more information, contact Greg Johnson, director of curriculum and instruction, Bering Strait School District, gjohnson@bssd.org, (907) 624-4279.

Figure 3.9: Sample K–12 Snapshot From Lake and Peninsula School District

	Levels											
	L1	L2	L3	L4	L5	L6	L7	L8	L9	L10	L11	L12
Reading					A	A	A	A	++	–		
Writing					A	A	A	P	++			
Math					A	A	A	A	A	A	++	
Social Studies		A	P	A	P	++						
Science		A	A	A	A							
Technology				A	A	A	++					
Cultural Awareness				A	A	A	++					
Personal/ Social/ Health				A	A	A	A	A				
Career Development		A	A	A	A	P	++					
Service Learning		A	A	A	A	A	A	++				

Achievement Levels: A = Advanced   P = Proficient   ++ = Developing   – = Emerging

Graduation Requirements: L8 Reading, L8 Writing, L9 Math, L5 Social Studies, L4 Science, L8 Technology, L7 Cultural Awareness, L7 Personal/Social/Health, L7 Career Development, L7 Service Learning

Source: Lake and Peninsula School District, King Salmon, Alaska, 907.246.4200.

Putting it All Together: Early Graduation—From a Traditional to a RISC System

In a traditional system, early high school graduation is highly unlikely for all but a few students, typically exceptionally bright students or highly independent learners who already have the motivation and drive to succeed. However, overall, the traditional education system is geared to students spending 13 years in school, from approximately age 5 to age 18. Conversely, in a RISC system, early high school graduation is a distinct possibility for many more students compared to the traditional system, not because RISC students are inherently more capable, but because the system itself accelerates learning; students move ahead as soon as they have demonstrated competency in a particular developmental level. A flexible system like this is what Marzano (2006) calls a "porous" system:

In a completely porous system a student could work at any level in any subject area. The system would be totally porous in that (theoretically) a student could be working on the 2nd grade level in one subject area and the 10th grade level in another. In fact, in such a system, the term *grade level* would most probably be dropped in favor of the more generic term *level*. Although such a system would be ideal, it is probably difficult if not impossible to implement in most districts as they are currently designed. (p. 139)

In the prior passage, Marzano implies that a radical departure from the traditional schooling system is necessary in order to attain an "ideal" system. The RISC approach is such a system, one in which every student has an opportunity to take ownership of his or her education and reach graduation levels at a pace that is developmentally appropriate for that student. No student waits for the rest of the class; at the same time, no student is pushed into learning beyond his or her readiness for learning. In fact, a strength of the RISC approach is student ownership of the learning process. When students understand and own the RISC system, they are less likely to resist it. In fact, many become ambassadors and defenders of that system.

The fact that students in a RISC system can complete their K–12 education early means that gifted students—who can experience just as much boredom, frustration, and learning disabilities as the next student—typically do much better than gifted students in a traditional system. In a RISC system, advanced performance levels—beyond 12th grade—are available for students who have demonstrated proficiency in all of the levels required for high school graduation in a particular content area. In essence, the K–12 RISC system becomes a K–16 system.

In one sense, the RISC system is very simple: Instruction is individualized, and students move forward at their own pace. However, implementing the system is complex and requires strong commitment from all stakeholders. The standards-based elements of the RISC system—instruction, assessment, and grading and reporting, all of which are aligned with standards—are realized and sustained through three systemic components of the RISC Approach to Schooling: shared vision, leadership, and continuous improvement. These concepts and processes, discussed in the following sections, are found in many schools, but how they are played out and how they interact is distinct in RISC schools and districts.

Shared Vision

Shared Vision in a RISC System

1. The RISC shared vision process deliberately draws the community into the system.

2. The RISC shared vision process seeks to create a critical mass of ownership—75 to 80% of stakeholders—that will ensure the effectiveness and sustainability of the RISC Approach to Schooling.

3. Following the RISC shared vision process with fidelity means that the views and ideas of individuals from the widest circle of a district's sphere of influence are sought.

4. The partnership of all stakeholders is important in schools and districts adopting the RISC model, but parent support is critical.

Shared vision is a widely touted concept in education. In fact, it is relatively common to see a set of goals or a mission statement posted in the central office of just about any school district in the country. The issue is that few complete the shared vision process fully, deeply, and with fidelity, and few use the shared vision to drive change.

What exactly is a shared vision, and why is it so important to the implementation of the RISC approach? Briefly, a shared vision is a set of goals—expressed as focus areas or as locally developed academic standards as well as cross-disciplinary, life-skills standards—along with specific action steps, that capture the perspectives of stakeholders about how best to educate students in the community and raise student achievement. Said another way, it is the education community speaking as one voice about the skills and knowledge that all students should acquire, the purposes and outcomes of schooling, the educational values of stakeholders, and how all of these will be realized over time.

The great value of the RISC shared vision process is that the community is deliberately drawn into the system and any walls between the school and the community come down. Bringing stakeholders together in this way—and continually involving them in the school or district over the long run—helps the community move from what might be disparate, disinterested, potentially conflicting groups of stakeholders to a unified, involved, supportive, and synergistic team, a true community working together for the sake of students. An essential aspect of this community building is empowering and inspiring the adults. So many adults as well as children do not believe in themselves. The RISC approach is about helping students find their spark, but it is also about inspiring adults as well. As RISC's Executive Director Wendy Battino explains, "This movement is about the kids, but along the way we found that it necessarily encompasses inspiring community members, school and district staff, and business leaders that they can make a difference by doing the right thing. In a very real way, I am a cheerleader for individuals to believe in their power and use it to make a difference."

The term *shared vision* is deliberately used relative to the RISC approach to make an important point about the effectiveness and longevity of initiatives involving deep change. The most effective shared vision process results in stakeholder *ownership* rather than stakeholder *buy-in*. Although the terms often are used interchangeably, ownership is quite different from buy-in. Buy-in means that stakeholders accept the plan, support it, understand it, and may see its value, but this does not necessarily equate to deep ownership. Ownership means that stakeholders view the goals and path of change *as their own*. Ultimately, the goal is to ensure that there is a critical mass of stakeholders—75 to 80%—who embrace the system as their own. Any school reform initiative, particularly one of RISC's magnitude, is much more likely to be sustained over the long run if it has parent and stakeholder support at this scale.

Schools and districts, like all organizations, have bursts of success or "pockets of excellence." For instance, average student scores may rise in math; or students in a third-grade teacher's classroom may do better over time than students in another third-grade teacher's classroom. In many school systems, these highs and lows tend to impact staff commitment to change: When scores are rising, it is easier to maintain the momentum of a school improvement initiative. When scores lag, it is tempting to change approaches, often midstream. But real, lasting change takes time and commitment—for any improvement endeavor.

At one end of the buy-in to ownership spectrum is the mission statement developed by a principal or superintendent. How this often plays out in practice is that the administrator stands up in a series of meetings and says, "Here is my vision. Let me share it with you." The administrator then prescribes the school or district's direction and focus.

A somewhat more effective approach—somewhere along the buy-in to ownership spectrum—occurs when planning and visioning are undertaken by a team of administrators who then solicit feedback from stakeholders about the proposed direction or plan. Gathering reactions and comments from teachers and others has some value, of course; however, at best the outcome is stakeholder agreement or buy-in. This partial involvement of stakeholders is a critical error because buy-in and support will be luke-warm at best, and true ownership will be out of reach. When challenges arise along the way, stakeholder support will be easily shaken. A failure to ensure authentic participation from a school or district's stakeholder groups is also a missed opportunity. Further, stakeholders who are not authentically involved from the beginning are very likely to become the strongest resisters.

At the highest end of the buy-in to ownership spectrum is the RISC shared vision process, which involves gathering stakeholders together and *collectively* creating a path for reform. The most successful individuals and organizations have a learner mindset; they welcome alternate viewpoints, healthy discussion, and even criticism. The highest outcome possible from following the RISC shared vision process with fidelity is deep, lasting ownership and commitment. Stakeholders engaged in this way will stand shoulder to shoulder with administrators.

This is particularly true of parents who have a highly personal stake in education in the community. The partnership of all stakeholders is important in schools and districts adopting the RISC model, but parent support is critical—and it is easy to see why. The simplest thing for parents to do, the path of least resistance, is to enroll their students in a traditional school, one whose process is familiar and where the academic bar is relatively easy for students to attain. A RISC school requires much, much more—of students and of parents. When parents are part of the creation process from day one, and come to see how the transformation will help their children, they become some of the strongest advocates.

Clearly, creating a shared vision must be a grassroots process; however, school and district leaders have an important role to play in ensuring that parents and other stakeholders make *educated, informed decisions* about schooling, and that the most effective shared vision for the future is created. School leaders must keep their eyes on the future, analyze market trends, review the latest research, and then share this information regularly and consistently with stakeholders.

The RISC Shared Vision Process

The shared vision process involves a number of steps:

1. **Meet.** Schedule numerous opportunities for discussion and debate among stakeholders. Invite stakeholders to take on specific leadership roles.

2. **Share information.** Share relevant research findings and trend data.

3. **Question and discuss.** Pose questions to spark conversation and critical thinking about student achievement and the future of the school or district.

4. **Synthesize.** Synthesize ideas into focus areas.

5. **Set goals.** Use the focus areas to identify detailed school- or district-wide goals.

6. **Write standards and assessments.** Write district standards and standards-based assessments based on stakeholder input.

7. **Develop an improvement plan.** Develop a systematic improvement plan, aligned across all levels of the system. Tap into the multitude of ways in which a diverse community of individuals,

with varying backgrounds, interests, career specialties, and areas of knowledge can enrich the academic life of the school.

8. **Continually improve.** Continually revisit, strengthen, and refine every aspect of the shared vision.

After gathering stakeholders together, the shared vision process begins by asking leading questions to engage stakeholders and elicit honest reflection and opinion. When the process is followed with the most fidelity, the views of individuals from the widest circle of a school's sphere of influence are sought. This sphere of influence includes not only administrators and teachers, but students, parents, support staff, and board members. Also included are business and community leaders, and staff members from facilities, maintenance, food services, transportation, and budgeting. Figure 3.10 (page 109) lists examples of questions that might be used to initiate conversation, as well as questions to pose after a preliminary set of goals, standards, and a related action plan have been developed.

Building a Team for the Long Haul

One of the immediate challenges of building a collective view for the future is understanding the varying perspectives of group members. As RISC staff members, coalition districts, and board members have worked with districts and schools interesting in adopting the RISC approach, they have found that there are three broad categories of individuals within any group:

- Omnivores

- Show Me's

- NFWs

As the term implies, *omnivores* are hungry for information. They constantly ask questions. Their refrain is, "Give me more. Show me how this works." These individuals are ready for change, ready for improvement. In fact, they are ready to go—right now. They pull the change toward them.

Figure 3.10: Shared Vision—Sample Questions

Shared Vision: Sample Questions
• What is working well in our school or district?
• What is incomplete, unresolved, or unsettled that is in the way of moving ahead?
• According to current research and our own data, how are our students doing—academically, personally, and socially?
• What happens to our students once they leave our K–12 system? How can we improve the ways in which we prepare them for this transition?
• How can we challenge students in ways they have not been challenged in the past?
• What will students need to know and be able to do to be successful in life, in the workplace of the 21st century, and in their future education?
• What new technologies, programs, or innovations can we use to help our students achieve at higher levels?
• What changes, if any, are needed to ensure that our system meets the needs of all students?
As the shared vision is solidified, a school or district might ask the following questions:
• Do we have a common set of goals?
• Did we obtain strong, representative stakeholder input to set the goals?
• Do stakeholders view the goals as their own?
• Can stakeholders articulate the goals to others?
• Are there specific, measurable action plans or action steps to implement those goals?
• Do we have a plan for using data to measure progress?
• Do we have a process for continually revisiting and refining our goals?

The *show me's* are on the fence. These individuals ask good questions, but it is clear they are thinking and processing what they are hearing. They may be avoiding making a commitment to the path of change, or may simply want more information.

The individuals who are most resistant, at least initially, to adopting the RISC model are the NFWs. Their view might be summed up as, "There is 'no frigging way' this is going to work." They may be frustrated, cynical, distrustful, resistant to change of any kind, or simply not sure how the changes will work in practice.

Teachers who initially are very skeptical of the RISC model frequently are the best teachers because they have been doing similar things in their classrooms, often on their own. They have been engaging students, encouraging them to take ownership of the learning process, establishing clear goals with students, trying to measure student progress specifically and more frequently, studying assessment results and other data, and so on. The RISC philosophy calls on them to take these things to the next level, which may seem to threaten how they have been doing things. Other teachers who initially are vocal critics may simply not see how it will all work, but because they are willing to be engaged, they often have the deepest understanding in the long run and become vocal advocates.

The courageous superintendents, principals, and other school leaders who take the bold steps required to implement the RISC Approach to Schooling must help parents and other stakeholders see the value of going down this path of change. Coming to understand and embrace—and be inspired by—this new approach is a transformational experience for everyone. As an administrator with the Chugach School District, and later as he has led other organizations adopting the RISC model, Rich DeLorenzo has found that taking community members through this process takes at least 3 days; in the end, the toughest critics often turn out to be the model's biggest supporters. As he says:

> They have to see it, experience it, and see it modeled for them. I've had community members, initially hardened and angry, become very emotional when they see what we can do to help children. They know their students need help and they don't know what to do with them. They don't know how to help them. We give them hope. They end up being part of the solution rather than the problem.

Ongoing Community Building

Developing and maintaining a solid, lasting relationship with the community is an ongoing journey. In communities with a history of a disconnected or poor relationship with the school or district, the new relationship may be fragile for some time. Unique approaches to healing and strengthening community relationships may be needed.

In Alaska's Chugach School District, for example, many Alaska Natives were angry (and rightfully so) about the ways in which their culture and language had been dishonored in the past. "When I went to school, we were treated poorly," they said. "We could not speak our language. We could not honor our culture."

As Chugach assistant superintendent at the time, Rich held a number of healing sessions during community meetings, asking for the community's forgiveness for the actions of previous school leaders. "We're here to help your students," he said. "You've trusted us with your children. We take that responsibility seriously." These community gatherings helped the seeds of the new relationship between school and community take root. As a result, many villagers now say, "You have resurrected who we are as a people. You value who we are."

Leadership

Leadership in a RISC System

1. The successful implementation of the RISC Approach to Schooling depends on a new breed of leaders whose primary focus is serving students rather than implementing policies.

2. Strong leadership at the top—from superintendents and principals—is imperative, but leadership and shared responsibility must be cultivated across all levels of the organization.

3. Teachers are critical, active partners in a RISC system.

4. Transforming and re-aligning a system to the RISC philosophy is second-order change, which can be profoundly unsettling. Superintendents, principals, and other school leaders must be skilled in leading this type of change process.

5. In a RISC system, leadership is defined, taught, measured, and reported based on the characteristics of leaders of second-order change.

6. The success of the RISC approach depends on leaders who dem-
    onstrate unwavering commitment and a strong sense of moral
    purpose.

The influence of good leadership on any system or organization cannot
be underestimated. Whether in business, the nonprofit sector, our children's
softball team, or the classroom, effective leaders guide, inspire, and lead.
Meaningful, deep, and lasting change in education, the kind of change the
RISC model makes possible, depends not only on leaders, but on a new
breed of leaders.

> "Leadership is where it begins and ends. If you don't have
> leadership to initiate this journey, it will never happen. If you
> don't have the capacity to build leadership from everyone—
> teachers, administrators, students, school board members, and
> so on—it will never be sustained."
>
> —Rich DeLorenzo

In today's global, technology-driven society, argues Heifetz (1994),
leaders must be prepared to think on their feet and to "[mobilize] people
to tackle tough problems" (p. 21). Heifetz also asserts that leadership is
not about having all the answers, but rather about a willingness to "face
problems for which there are no simple, painless solutions" (p. 21). Yet,
traditional adminstrator education programs continue to focus on growing good *managers*—principals and superintendents who may know how
to choose a promising reading program, arrange bus schedules, and balance budgets, but who often are at a loss when it comes to driving lasting,
comprehensive, meaningful change.

Most superintendents and principals are inefficient as leaders not
because of a lack of desire to be good leaders, but because of the nature of
the education system itself. The condition and culture of education might
be summed up as, "manage crisis, comply with federal and state mandates,
and avoid risk." It is very challenging to break out of that paradigm.

However, in order to effect deep and lasting change, breaking out of
that paradigm is essential. Leaders must develop what Charlotte Roberts
(2000) refers to as "a 'learner-centered' as opposed to an 'authority-centered'

approach to all problems, inside and outside the classroom" (p. 416). In an authority-centered system, says Roberts, "teaching is organized for the adults in the system—in the same way that . . . leadership is organized for the sake of the administrator's self-image" (p. 417).

In a RISC learner-centered system, the primary concern is serving students. These superintendents, principals, curriculum directors, and other leaders realize that there are things that they know are right to do for students, but no one else is doing these things—in fact, many people say they should *not* be doing them. RISC's student-centered focus is realized through *shared leadership*.

Shared Leadership and Capacity Building: Building a Team of Innovators

When most of us think of a school or district leader, we think of someone in the top position, specifically, a superintendent or principal. Strong, unwavering leadership from superintendents and principals is critical, to be sure, but when school reform efforts are affiliated too closely with one or two individuals, the entire effort is in danger of falling apart. Indeed, our collective addiction to what Senge and his colleagues (1999) call "the myth of the hero-leader" (p. 11) may be part of the reason reform efforts fail:

> In effect, the myth of the hero-leader creates a reinforcing vicious spiral of dramatic changes imposed from the top, and diminished leadership capacity in the organization, leading eventually to new crises and yet more heroic leaders. (pp. 11–12)

Success, sustainability, and the innovative climate that is crucial to the RISC model depend on much more than strong leaders at the top. As Michael Fullan (2005) writes, "Sustainability is a team sport, and the team is large" (p. 29).

Schools and districts that adopt the RISC Approach to Schooling undergo a dramatic shift in how they view leadership. Directives and other one-way communication require little or nothing of a leader in the way of dialogue and debate, mentoring, guidance, and team building. But those superintendents and principals who take the path of developing shared responsibility for success—and the capacity to realize this success—will find the task of guiding the system through the rough waters of change much easier and infinitely more effective in the long run.

A number of education theorists and researchers have written about the importance of developing shared leadership, also distinguished as leadership capacity across an organization, leadership communities, and a community of leaders (see, for example, Lambert, 1998, 2002; Senge et al., 1999; Sergiovanni, 1994). Shared leadership must be built in the front office and beyond, from administrators and teachers, to students, parents, and support staff. The reform effort must transcend individuals.

In a RISC system, teachers are perhaps the primary group of stakeholders among whom to develop shared leadership. The RISC approach requires much of teachers in terms of engagement, ownership, innovation, and responsibility. Shared leadership means that teachers experience themselves as partners in the change effort. They are not sitting back, waiting for directions or instruction from curriculum directors, principals, superintendents, or others "on high." Rather, they are offering ideas for improvement across the school or district, making instructional decisions that they are empowered by district administrators to make, being creative and innovative, and working collaboratively with their colleagues. In other words, they are responsible, full partners in leading the school or district to implement lasting improvements that directly impact individual student achievement.

Leadership for Second-Order Change

Many large-scale school improvement initiatives start out strong, but lose steam as the magnitude of the change and the level of commitment required become apparent. For example, in a study undertaken by the Cross City Campaign for Urban School Reform (2005) of school reform initiatives in Chicago, Milwaukee, and Seattle, it became apparent that resources, professional development, data use, and leadership were not enough in and of themselves to effect lasting change. What was missing in these large-scale school reform initiatives was leadership that ensured that connections were made between district-level goals and actual classroom practice.

Relative to leadership, Marzano et al. (2005) point to a principal reason for these kinds of failures:

> The leadership supporting an innovation must be consistent with the order of magnitude of the change represented by the innovation. If the leadership techniques do not match the order of change required by an innovation, the innovation will probably fail regardless of its merits. (p. 66)

As noted in chapter 1, second-order change—the kind of change associated with the RISC Approach to Schooling—can be profoundly unsettling. Leading this type of change requires new skills and processes, but more important, dramatically different ways of thinking, what Fullan (1993) calls a "fundamental shift of mind":

> Without such a shift of mind the insurmountable basic problem is the juxtaposition of a continuous change *theme* with a continuous *conservative system*. On the one hand, we have the constant and ever expanding presence of educational innovation and reform. . . . On the other hand, however, we have an educational system which is fundamentally conservative. The way that teachers are trained, the way that schools are organized, the way that the educational hierarchy operates, and the way that education is treated by political decision-makers results in a system that is more likely to retain the *status quo* than to change. When change is attempted in such circumstances it results in defensiveness, superficiality or at best short-lived pockets of success. (p. 3)

School leaders overseeing incremental changes in their schools or districts, such as the implementation of a new curriculum in a single content area, do not need to be dynamic leaders. But when the proposed change has dramatic implications at all levels of the school system, such as shifting from an A–F grading system to a standards-based system or instituting a performance-based pay system for teachers, school leaders need to draw on a different set of skills and aptitudes. In other words, they need to make a "fundamental shift of mind."

Although we have learned a great deal about how to develop strong leaders, we have not yet figured out, as an education community and as a nation, how to translate that learning into practice on a larger scale. In other words, we have not taken the time to collectively define what good leadership means. As a result, the leadership evaluation tools in today's schools vary little from those of a decade ago. This lack of a firm definition and parallel evaluation tools makes it difficult not only to *measure* good leadership, but to *refine* it—to continuously review what works and what does not.

In a RISC system, leadership is defined, taught, measured, and reported based on the characteristics of leaders of second-order change (see, for example, Marzano et al., 2005). These indicators of strong leadership are embedded into evaluation processes for teachers, principals, superintendents, and school board members, evaluated annually, and refined.

For schools and districts undergoing the paradigm shift from a time-based, teacher- and textbook-driven system to RISC's standards-based, student-centered system, success will depend in large measure on the qualities and actions of school leaders. What, then, are the characteristics of leaders that will ensure that the new system is sustainable?

Based on a survey of education leaders, Marzano (2007) identified a number of practices in which leaders must be skilled in order to lead second-order change processes:

- Shaking up the status quo
- Expecting some new things to seem worse
- Proposing new ideas
- Operating from strong beliefs
- Tolerating ambiguity and dissent
- Talking research and theory
- Creating explicit goals for change
- Defining success in terms of goals

Leadership and Moral Purpose

All of the leadership practices included in this list are action oriented. It is relatively easy for a superintendent or principal to say all the right things, to stand up at a school board meeting or PTA meeting and talk about a new program or how things should change. Inspiring stakeholders by speaking about change is vitally important, but it is not enough to simply talk about great ideas, plans, and hopes for the future. For a school or district to make the fundamental changes that are at the heart of the RISC approach—changes that challenge status-quo thinking and well-entrenched ways of doing things—leaders must partner their words with meaningful action and then stand by those actions.

Shifting to the RISC philosophy can bring up resistance and dissent from everyone and anyone: teachers, parents, students, community members, board members—you name it. Even some of those who were originally on board may become less enthusiastic over time in the face of stagnant scores, disgruntled parents, a divided community, or students not graduating with their age peers. Around every corner is a reason for the ordinary leader to stop, backpedal, pull back, or retreat to business as usual. When the going gets tough, school leadership typically falls apart and momentum is lost. Penetrating the view that "this is how we have always done it" can be, says one of the leaders of an Alaska school using the RISC approach, like "cracking a block of cement."

It is critical, especially in fragmented communities, to send a strong message that school leaders will stick with the mission even when they are challenged, even when responses from parents or community members seem unfair or unwarranted. School leaders are needed who have the courage to stay true to the shared vision, strategies, and agreed-upon action steps, even if it means putting their careers on the line.

RISC leaders are individuals who are willing to take a radically different approach to schooling than they have in the past, and who have the courage and moral purpose necessary to see the vision through. As Michael Fullan (2003) writes, "Moral purpose of the highest order is having a system where all students learn, the gap between high and low performance becomes greatly reduced, and what people learn enables them to be successful" (p. 29).

That is precisely what superintendents, principals, and other leaders in RISC districts do repeatedly over time. They do not simply talk about what they are going to do or what they would like to do. They have the courage and fortitude to take actions that may be viewed unfavorably because they are clear about the moral direction that guides these actions; they take steps that are in the service of a greater goal. The evolving stories of RISC districts are replete with examples of these kinds of leaders. "Our journey has not been about doing what is comfortable," says John Davis, retired superintendent for Bering Strait School District. "It's been about doing what is really *un*comfortable."

In 2003–2004, the third year of implementing the RISC model, the resolve of Lake and Peninsula School District leaders to stick with the new system was tested when several students who would have graduated under the old system were not granted diplomas. There was a huge outcry from parents, and the new standards-based system was attacked.

But Superintendent Steve Atwater held firm and refused to back down. Atwater's refusal to relent in the face of criticism, upset, and controversy is a prime example of the qualities needed to lead a group of individuals through the challenges of second-order change—what Marzano et al. (2005) call a "willingness to temporarily upset a school's equilibrium" (p. 44).

This kind of action separates true leaders from those who are leaders in name only. As a teacher, a principal, a superintendent, or a school board member, are you willing to stand your ground?

Standing firm and tolerating dissent, while also inspiring ownership, requires something more of school leaders. This combination of attributes sets the RISC leader apart from other kinds of leaders. Roger Sampson and Rich DeLorenzo, recalls RISC's Executive Director Wendy Battino, were two such exceptional leaders of the Chugach School District:

> Rich and Roger were taking heat. Many teachers were giving them grief. It was painful making the switch to the new system. But Rich and Roger stuck to their guns and were so confident: "This is what we're doing." There was no room for a wedge. In

other districts, people complain and leadership falters and tries to accommodate, rather than lead.

The great example Rich and Roger set was that they stood their ground, but did so in a way that generated ownership from teachers, students, parents, and the community. They created a vision for education reform, student success, and community transformation that inspired and challenged everyone at the same time.

A Vision for Leadership Beyond Yourself

"The highest good of leadership is when it is based on a vision of something beyond yourself as a superintendent or principal, something to be true to, something that compels you to sacrifice your personal interests and needs.

"It's about modeling altruism. It's got to be about the vision of people beyond me, who come after me, making it happen. Leaders like Mother Teresa, St. Francis, and Martin Luther King—none of them was perfect—but they all had a deep passion and vision to make the world a better place.

"As a leader your focus must be, 'Whoever comes behind me will be better than I've been.' It can't be about any of us as individuals. It has to be about the vision. I've seen so many innovations come and go that were driven by personalities. Rarely have they been successful."

—Rich DeLorenzo

Continuous Improvement

Continuous Improvement in a RISC System

1. Nothing in a RISC system is stagnant. Change and improvement are constants.

2. Continuous improvement is synonymous with the RISC Approach to Schooling.

3. A RISC system encourages both introspection and innovation.

4. RISC's continuous improvement process—vision, implement, study, act—can be used at the individual and organizational levels.

A core process always at play in any RISC system is continuous improvement. Indeed, nothing in a RISC system is stagnant; change and improvement are constants. The commitment to continuous improvement permeates everything and affects everyone in a RISC system. As Highland Tech High's Principal Mark Standley says so well, "Because perfection is impossible, continuous improvement is our only viable option." The continuous improvement cycle is vital to ensuring that a school or district's focus and direction are fresh, that they continually reflect the latest lessons learned, and that details are integrated that may have been missed along the way.

Good teachers are always focused on how to do things better, reach students more effectively, and make learning more meaningful. The problem in many traditional education systems does not lie with individual teachers; the problem lies with the nature and culture of the system itself.

Many schools and districts, for example, do a wonderful job of creating elaborate strategic plans, but when it comes to implementing or refining these plans, most fall short. In fact, often within a week or so of creating a plan for improvement, those who were involved in the planning process see little connection between the plan they just spent days developing and what is happening in individual classrooms and the school or district as a whole. Further, improvement efforts in many school systems tend to be infrequent—perhaps every 5 years, when it becomes clear that student achievement data do not measure up to strategic planning goals. The reaction in these instances is often simply to dump whatever program is in use and adopt something new.

This reactive approach occurs because most school systems lack a clear set of shared tools and processes for continuous improvement. Individual teachers may find effective ways of continually improving their classroom instruction, but there is no formal, shared, systemic, ongoing process for *all* teachers to improve, and no ongoing conversations about what teachers are doing and what they can do to improve.

This lack of shared ongoing processes for improvement results in a culture of mediocrity, of taking the easiest route. Teachers and other staff members end up doing the same thing day after day, week after week—

whatever is easiest. In short, in many school systems refinement and growth are haphazard. Improvements, when they are made, are frequently the result of happenstance or reacting to crisis, rather than being proactive. What is missing in many education systems is a deliberate, focused, systemic, and systematic approach to continuous improvement that creates a climate for ongoing refinement, innovation, and creativity.

A standards-based, student-centered approach—one designed to make it possible for every student to excel to the highest possible levels—is inextricably entwined with the principle of ongoing improvement. In fact, it might be said that the RISC Approach to Schooling and continuous improvement are synonymous.

The continuous improvement aspect of the RISC model helps ensure accountability by relentlessly documenting the journey of continuous improvement, even when it is uncomfortable or difficult to do so. As shown in Figure 3.11, the RISC continuous improvement process is defined by four characteristics based in best practice.

Figure 3.11: Characteristics of RISC's Continuous Improvement Process

Characteristics of RISC's Continuous Improvement Process
1. **Cyclical and ongoing**—Stakeholders commit to an ongoing process that cycles from vision to implementation to study to action, and back to vision again.
2. **Systematic**—Proven, clear tools and processes are in place for continuous improvement (for example, plus-delta charts, affinity diagrams, root-cause analysis processes, and brainstorming processes). What the individual "great teacher" does can be replicated by all teachers.
3. **Systemic**—Continuous improvement tools and processes are aligned vertically, reaching across all levels of the school system from administrators to teachers to support staff. Administrators and teachers are on the same page, rather than at odds or disconnected from one another.
4. **Formal**—The continuous improvement process is a formal process that uses data to regularly and consistently assess every element of the teaching and learning process, including standards, instructional strategies, assessments, and reporting tools, as well as the shared vision and strategic plans that guide the overall educational process.

What does all of this mean in practice? A RISC culture of excellence is characterized by the following practices:

- Teachers and administrators track student achievement and are always searching for better ways to accelerate student achievement.

- Teachers continually re-evaluate and improve their lesson plans.

- Teachers collaborate and share effective strategies, creating a professional learning community that supports staff growth and development.

- Every staff member follows a process for improvement, which includes setting goals, continually re-evaluating progress, and making ongoing refinements as needed.

- Administrators, teachers, and other school staff regularly revisit and strengthen every aspect of the system—standards and developmental levels, common assessments, grading and reporting processes, budgeting for school improvement, relationships among stakeholders, communication with parents, and so on.

RISC schools and districts are very much data driven. District and school leaders regularly review student achievement results (both short-term and trend data), surveys of teacher satisfaction, and indicators of community support to evaluate the organization's success in reaching identified goals. When the results are less than stellar or data indicate that one or more goals may not be realized, questions arise: How could we be more innovative? What do we need to do to meet—and exceed—our goals? In short, the continuous improvement process encourages introspection and innovation.

Vision, Implement, Study, Act

A characteristic of high-performing organizations is the use of some kind of continuous improvement process. This process is most often referred to as a PDSA cycle for **p**lan, **d**o, **s**tudy, **a**ct. RISC's process is referred to as the VISA cycle—**v**ision, **i**mplement, **s**tudy, **a**ct (see Figure 3.12)—to call attention to the critical role of visioning:

- Define a shared **v**ision for improvement.

- **I**mplement the vision.

- **S**tudy the success of implementation.

- **A**ct on the results of the evaluation.

Figure 3.12: The VISA Cycle

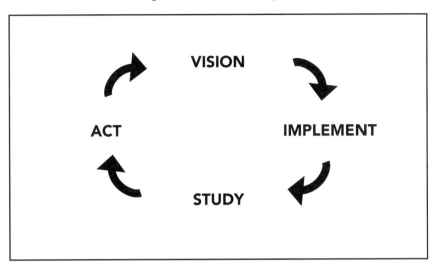

Like other continuous improvement cycles, RISC's VISA process can be used at the individual and organizational levels. The process can be used by administrators and by teachers—either individually or as teaching staff—and by students, school boards, and even entire districts. Figure 3.13 (pages 124–126) is an example of a district-level VISA process that is aligned vertically, from the district level to the classroom teacher level to the student level.

Figure 3.13: Sample Districtwide VISA
Continuous Improvement Process

District Level

Vision/Goal: Improve average student reading scores by 10% on the statewide test within 1 year.

Implement the Vision—Action Plan:

1. Conduct a data analysis concerning students' relative strengths and weaknesses in decoding, fluency, and comprehensions.

2. Analyze our current deployment of reading instructional practices across the district.

3. Review guidance from research and from practitioners nationwide; benchmark district practices to research findings and best practices.

4. In collaboration with school administrators and teachers, determine direction and next steps to accelerate growth in student reading scores.

5. Conduct intensive training with all staff on next steps and reading program refinements or the elements of a new program if we determine that one should be adopted.

Study Implementation:

1. Monitor implementation of program changes to see how well they are being deployed.

Refine and Act:

Results indicate that students' comprehension skills continue to lag and that teachers are inconsistently deploying agreed-upon district reading practices.

1. Analyze reading comprehension practices in our schools.

2. Circle back to research and synthesize any new findings relative to reading comprehension.

3. Study strategies used by other districts to strengthen students' comprehension skills.

4. To address teachers' inconsistent use of reading comprehension strategies, begin collecting baseline data about the frequency and quality of classroom instructional practices.

5. Analyze these results for a new iteration of the VISA process.

Figure 3.13: Sample Districtwide VISA
Continuous Improvement Process *(continued)*

School Level

Vision/Goal: Improve average student reading scores by 10% on the statewide test within 1 year.

Implement—Action Plan:

1. Collect student achievement data relative to reading skills. Disaggregate and aggregate data.

2. Bring teachers together to commit to schoolwide strategies by signing a Reading Improvement Design. The design includes how students will be regularly assessed and clearly articulates strategies in decoding, fluency, and comprehension.

3. Hold discussions with staff about what works and what does not work, using leading questions to stimulate critical thinking (for example, "What is our definition of a good reader?").

4. Send information to the district office from our data analyses and outcomes of staff discussions.

5. Review and assess our own best practices. What strategies are those teachers using whose students are doing very well?

Study Implementation: Meet monthly as a staff to discuss and create a running journal of best practices. Meet every two months to administer analytical reading assessments.

Refine and Act: After one year, schoolwide student scores on the statewide tests have increased 15% in decoding, 21% in fluency, but only 6% in reading comprehension.

1. Continue to improve decoding scores and fluency scores with individual students.

2. Re-examine reading comprehension instructional practices and learning activities.

3. Disaggregate test scores to find the root cause of the problem.

4. Begin a new VISA process for next year.

Figure 3.13: Sample Districtwide VISA
Continuous Improvement Process *(continued)*

Classroom Teacher Level

Vision/Goal: Improve average student reading achievement by 10% on the statewide test.

Implement the Vision—My Action Plan:

1. Monitor individual students' knowledge and skill in decoding, fluency, and comprehension.

2. Track individual student progress and share results with students.

3. Empower students to track their own progress.

4. Work with my colleagues to learn what they are doing that works; refine my instructional practices.

Study Implementation: Administer reading test after 2 weeks to see if instructional changes have influenced students' reading skills.

Refine and Act: Identify instructional strategies and activities needed for different students.

Student Level

Vision/Goal: Improve my reading scores on the next test by 10% compared to my scores on the last test within 1 year.

Implement the Vision—My Action Plan:

1. Meet with my teacher to review my strengths and weaknesses in decoding, fluency, and comprehension.

2. Write weekly goals for each area.

3. Review my goals each morning.

4. Create a daily strategy to work on my goals.

5. Create a chart to track my progress in each area.

6. Refine my goals each afternoon.

7. After each test, meet with my teacher, review my progress, and revise my goals as needed.

Study Implementation: At the end of each week, ask myself, "Did I accomplish the goals I set out to accomplish? If not, what did I do? What didn't I do?"

Revise and Act: At the end of each week, make adjustments in my strategies depending on how I evaluate my progress.

4

Replication: Successes, Lessons Learned, and Suggested Action Steps

Leading Questions

1. Can you replicate an educational system that involves changing our most fundamental approaches to schooling?

2. What are the chances of sustaining a system that represents such deep change?

3. What are the pitfalls and opportunities of replication?

As word of RISC's mission and its student-centered, performance-based philosophy has spread, schools and districts across Alaska (and a growing number in the Lower 48 states) have made an official commitment to transition to the RISC Approach to Schooling. This chapter highlights the lessons learned by these early adopters of the RISC model.

The deep changes that accompany adoption of the RISC approach can be difficult and unsettling; when challenges arise, it can be tempting to discard the model instead of grappling with difficult questions. One of the most well-organized supports for systems to stay the course through the replication process is the Re-Inventing Schools Coalition.

As described in chapter 2, the Re-Inventing Schools Coalition (see www.reinventingschools.org) is a nonprofit organization dedicated to replicating the RISC model and supporting other schools and districts as they move through this process. Fundamentally, it is also a coalition of the districts and schools that are replicating the RISC approach. By creating a formal alliance of the organizations implementing the model, the collaboration process that the Chugach School District used so effectively to inspire synergism and innovative thinking was expanded. The coalition is a reflection of the idea that "two minds are better than one." In this case, many minds—focused on a shared goal—are better than a few.

The coalition serves a number of purposes. It unites those school sites that are replicating the model; serves as a network for sharing tools, processes, and lessons learned; and provides guidance and support to districts and schools interested in adopting the RISC model. The coalition also empowers other organizations to make the model their own and, over time, to become independent leaders and coaches in their own right for other school sites. Finally, the coalition helps ensure that the model is replicated with fidelity, the surest way to the realization of sustainable improvements.

As schools and districts join the coalition, they agree, in turn, to collaborate and to share information, successes and failures, and tools and processes. In addition, each of the coalition members has put in place a number of core supports and specific plans, including the following:

- A school board resolution committing to implementation of the RISC Approach to Schooling

- An action plan, with measurable evaluation criteria, outlining the specific steps the organization is taking to adopt the model

- A commitment to seeking and obtaining a waiver from the state Carnegie unit requirement for high school programs

- A systematic process for ensuring that all stakeholders—students, teachers, parents, community members, school board members, and administrators—know what the RISC approach is and what it entails

- A systematic process for regularly soliciting stakeholder input regarding systemwide goals

The RISC Change Continuum: Moving to a Student-Centered, Standards-Based System

As schools and districts transition from their existing systems to a RISC system, they are likely to move through six stages of change, or levels of implementation:

1. **Awareness**—We are aware of the need for this process.

2. **Understanding**—We understand how to do this process.

3. **First implementation**—We have implemented this process.

4. **Routine use**—We routinely use this process.

5. **Refinement**—We continuously refine this process.

6. **Replication**—We teach other districts and organizations to replicate this process.

Full implementation of the RISC model typically is a multiyear process; we suggest that systems follow a 3- to 5-year timeline, roughly shown in Figure 4.1. The length of time needed to scale up to full implementation of the model depends, to a degree, on the size of the system. Smaller districts, which face fewer challenges relative to scale, can generally reach full, systemwide implementation within 3 years. In larger districts, this process can take as long as 5 years. Regardless of system size, we encourage systems committed to the approach to garner deep ownership, complete the planning process, and ramp up as quickly as possible to mitigate the potential negative effects of attrition of key leadership that occurs in any system.

Figure 4.1: RISC Change Continuum Replication Timeline

	Year 1	Year 2	Year 3	Year 4	Year 5
Awareness	▨				
Understanding	▨				
First Implementation		▨			
Routine Use		▨	▨		
Refinement			▨	▨	
Replication			▨	▨	▨

Schools and districts will move through the phases of change with varying degrees of speed, and their experiences will likely be quite different, depending on the culture of the system. The RISC Approach to Schooling may, for example, be met with resistance, with cautious interest, or with great enthusiasm. Nonetheless, there are general guidelines and actions to take within each phase. Figure 4.2 provides a broad overview of these steps for both small and large systems. RISC schools will typically experience their first successes at the midpoint of the 3- to 5-year implementation process. By this time, the district will have built leadership capacity, created a strong based of ownership among stakeholders, and developed strong assessments aligned with the district's standards. This will create more time to focus on refining and strengthening processes and approaches.

Figure 4.2: Three- to Five-Year Ramp-Up to Full Implementation of RISC Model

Small Systems	Large Systems
1,000 or fewer students, usually with 3 elementary, 1 middle, and 1 high school	40,000 or more students, usually with 50 elementary, 15 middle, and 7–8 high schools
Year 1: Study and Preparation	
Small system: Year 1 activities may be accomplished in as little as 1 or 2 months.	**Large system:** Year 1 activities may take 6 to 9 months.

Small or large system:

- Form a leadership team to guide, oversee, and facilitate transition to a RISC system.

- Create the need as well as the opportunity: Conduct a thorough needs assessment. Create a shared vision for the future, both in terms of what is taught and how it is taught.

- Benchmark current practices against best practices. Share this information with stakeholders to help them make educated, informed decisions.

- Identify gaps between the present and the future.

- Review, strengthen, and/or build the basics: standards, aligned assessments, standards-based grading and reporting processes, and so on.

- Create a detailed plan for how the model will be implemented over the long term across the district at all grade levels for all content areas. Strategize and make decisions about the specifics of implementation for years 2, 3, and beyond.

- Begin to align courses and scheduling with standards and graduation requirements.

Year 2: Implement/Ramp-Up Based on Year 1 Decisions

Small or large system: Refine alignment of courses and scheduling with standards and graduation requirements. Near year end, revisit implementation plans created during year 1, and the nuts and bolts of the system (such as standards, end-of-level assessments, and report cards) in those content areas and grade levels where the model is already being implemented. Revise and refine all as needed. Contact other RISC schools and districts for lessons learned, strengths, and opportunities for improvement.

Small system ramp-up options:	Large system ramp-up options:
- In core content areas only (for example, reading, writing, and math) - At a few grade levels - Across the entire district, K–12	- Vertical slice (for example, a geographic area of 4 elementary schools that feed into 1 middle school that feeds into 1 high school) - All elementary schools

Figure 4.2: Three- to Five-Year Ramp-Up to
Full Implementation of RISC Model *(continued)*

Year 3: Continue Ramp-Up; Continuous Improvement for Grade Levels and/or Schools Already Implementing	
Small system: Expand effort to the entire district, K–12, if Year 2 ramp-up was not systemwide.	**Large system:** Expand to other geographic areas or ramp-up to middle schools.
Year 4: Continuous Improvement and/or Ramp-Up	
Small or large system: Analyze school and district achievement data and modify deployment as needed.	
Small system: Continuous improvement in full swing, K–12	**Large system:** Ramp-up to high schools
Year 5: Continuous Improvement in Full Swing, K–12	
Small or large system: Support and guide other schools and districts. Continue to build leadership, and clarify and strengthen processes.	
Small system: Second year of continuous improvement, K–12	**Large system:** First year of continuous improvement, K–12

Lessons Learned

School systems that are farther along the 3- to 5-year change continuum have identified through trial and error a number of specific strategies to address the challenges that arose. The following lessons learned are by no means an exhaustive list, but rather a representative sample of what early adopters of the RISC model have learned:

- Take time to study, plan, prepare, and learn from others before officially implementing the model.

- Create a burning platform for change as well as the opportunity of change.

- Think beyond buy-in. Build deep commitment from at least 75–80% of stakeholders before moving forward.

- Prepare key personnel to lead second-order change.

- Adopt a high-quality standards-based grading and reporting software program.

- Develop a community of professionals—among teachers, administrators, board members, parents, and students—with a learner mindset.

- Prepare for the changing dynamics of graduation, both for students on track to meet graduation requirements early as well as those who need additional time.

- Begin the continuous improvement process early on.

Take Time to Study, Plan, Prepare, and Learn From Others

Superintendents, principals, teachers, policymakers, board members—essentially, anyone drawn to learn more about the RISC approach—may have come to a difficult realization: The current system is bankrupt and students are failing, or not reaching the high achievement levels they are capable of reaching. Yet, one of the most valuable lessons learned is that, despite the urgent need for change, it is imperative to take time for careful preparation, planning, and study. This is also the time to seek guidance and advice from experienced RISC systems, from the RISC organization itself, and from researchers and practitioners well-versed in standards-based processes.

Allocating a defined planning period—some RISC schools have spent up to a year—to study, learn, and create before anything is officially launched pays great dividends. Taking time to put as much as possible in place in advance—for example, a process for gaining stakeholder input, a plan for leadership training at all levels, a shared view of where the community is headed, agreed-upon standards, and procedures for deploying and evaluating standards and assessments—creates a foundation for implementation and provides valuable time for teachers, students, parents, and community members to prepare for the shift.

Year 1, the time for preparation and study, is also the time to develop a long-term plan for ramp-up at every level of the school or district, whether the "long term" occurs in 1 year or 5 years. Once this big-picture plan has been completed—at all grade levels, in all content areas, in all schools—the leadership team should strategize and make decisions about *when and how* the model will be implemented at each level, in each content area, and in each school in the system. They might ask themselves, "Which grade levels or schools should go first? Which content areas? What is feasible and when? To what extent are we prepared? How strong is our shared commitment? How strong is our leadership?"

A related step is to identify, to the extent possible, the *activities and details* of implementation for the first year of implementation (year 2 of a 3- to 5-year plan) and each subsequent year. This is the time, for instance:

- To write, or review and strengthen, standards across grade levels or developmental levels that stakeholders consider important for students to master in academic and nonacademic areas

- To develop end-of-level assessments aligned with those standards

- To put in place, or begin to put in place, a standards-based grading and reporting system

Any of these activities can be completed by a school or district team or contracted to an external organization skilled in these areas.

Ideally, the entire district will begin utilizing the model at the same time. However, a district may choose to delay implementation at the upper grades until some of the work at the lower grades has been completed. Making the shift to a RISC system can be more challenging in middle school and high school for a number of reasons. For one, education from grade 6 on is typically divided among different teachers who specialize in one or two content areas, and team or interdisciplinary teaching may be more or less present in one district versus another. In addition, as students move up, the stakes (particularly relative to high school graduation) become higher. For these reasons and more, implementing a standards- and performance-based approach at the upper grades may require additional planning and preparation.

Because of these dynamics, districts may choose to implement the RISC model in the lower grade levels first—for instance, kindergarten through grades 5 or 6. When the RISC system is up and running in these grade levels, district leaders can turn their attention to implementing the model in the upper grade levels. Another option, particularly for larger districts, is to implement in a K–12 vertical *slice* of the district, for example, in a few elementary schools that feed into one middle school that feeds into one high school. There are obvious downsides to this approach (such as potential miscommunication, lack of collegiality across the district, and confused or upset parents) as well as benefits (such as controlled implementation, and identification and minimization of problems). Smaller systems may decide to begin with several grade levels or content areas and then expand; however, implementing the model across all grades K–12 in 1 year is also quite possible, especially for highly focused districts.

Create a Burning Platform for Change as Well as the Opportunity of Change

The year 1 planning and preparation phase is a time of critical analysis along with inspirational visioning, which lays the foundation for implementation in years 2 and later. The impetus for transitioning to RISC's standards- and performance-based approach may initially arise as a result of "confronting the brutal facts" about student achievement. In other words, district leaders may have the sense of standing on a burning platform: There is a crisis afoot, and change cannot happen quickly enough. However, at the same time, it is important to create the *opportunity* for change. What does adopting this model make possible for students that has not yet been realized to date? What is now possible for the future of the school and the community, both locally and globally, that students will be part of and contribute to in the coming years? Operating inside a context of *crisis* is one motivator that pushes us to change what we have been doing, in a sense to change past practices and processes. Creating *a vision of what is possible* pulls us toward the future.

Think Beyond Buy-In: Develop Strong Stakeholder Ownership

As discussed more fully in the Shared Vision section of chapter 3, stakeholder buy-in is one of the goals of many school improvement initiatives. However, for a change of the magnitude involved in transitioning to the RISC model to be sustained over the long term and to fully realize student achievement gains, *buy-in* is simply not enough; the goal must be *ownership* and *partnership*—from at least 75 to 80% of stakeholders—driven by a shared vision of what is possible. There is little point in moving down the path of transformation, through the paradigm shift, without deep commitment and shared moral purpose. A few of the schools and districts that have undertaken the transition to the RISC standards- and performance-based approach have learned the hard way that weak stakeholder support is frequently an early indicator of failure in the long run. Indeed, deep commitment from leaders and stakeholders may be the lynchpin of successfully implementing and sustaining the RISC approach.

As any pioneer in any field knows, inventions are not always met with happy, unquestioning support. In fact, resistance, controversy, questioning, and skepticism are likely to flow quite freely—both from those who *welcome* invention and certainly from those who *resist* it—particularly when a new approach requires significant changes in behaviors and points of view. For this reason and many others, building and sustaining deep, long-lasting, strong stakeholder partnership must be a long-term, ongoing focus.

Strong communication lines among district leaders and stakeholder groups make a difference in any school or district, but this is especially the case in a RISC setting, which differs so fundamentally from the education system that is familiar to parents and students. Leaders must focus on developing stakeholder understanding, reinforcing this over time, and clarifying the distinctive processes and approaches that make the RISC model what it is.

Ensuring that communication is always at the highest levels helps alleviate confusion or misunderstanding that may arise. This is especially the case in RISC schools that are part of a district that may not be using the RISC model districtwide. Parents—even those who helped create the school's shared vision and implementation plans—may find themselves confused when district policy appears to conflict with school policy. Confusion may be further amplified when RISC parents speak with friends who have children enrolled in non-RISC district schools. School leaders must make it a priority to build personal, strong relationships with district staff to coordinate communication and answer questions. This important relationship building cannot be underestimated.

Processes and programs that engage students, parents, and others as a unified community can be powerful tools that also increase the likelihood of sustainability and a "win-win" experience for stakeholders and school leaders alike. For example, RISC schools might create a weekly gathering in which teachers, parents, and students advise the school principal on decisions regarding the quality of the school community.

Students are perhaps the most important and obvious group of individuals in which to encourage and develop deep ownership and shared leadership. In RISC settings, student participation, ownership, and leadership are quite high and demonstrated in a multitude of ways. For instance, visitors to Anchorage-based Highland Tech High are likely to be treated to a tour by a student. Student ownership of Highland Tech's educational model is so strong that the student tour guide speaks about the model as though she designed it herself. In the fall of 2007, students with the Bering Strait School District explained the RISC approach to a visiting educator from Queensland, Australia, and interviewed him about his preliminary perceptions of the approach; other district students made presentations at a state Association of School Administrators conference about various technologies they use in their education and gave personalized demonstrations after the presentation at the request of interested superintendents.

Prepare Key Personnel to Lead Second-Order Change

The success of every stage of adopting the RISC model depends in large measure on the caliber and strength of leadership. Year 1 is the time to ensure that those in administrative positions—the superintendent, principal or principals, and other key leaders—have the necessary skills, abilities, and mindset. As discussed in chapters 1 and 3, transitioning to the RISC approach is second-order change—change that no longer follows the step-by-step incremental, predicted path from the past, but is a dramatic departure from what was expected or anticipated. Second-order change—which shakes up the existing state of affairs, challenges underlying assumptions, and stimulates new thought—equates to a transformation of the primary operating principles, structure, and design of the education system.

School and district leaders of successful second-order change must have an entirely different set of skills and aptitudes at their disposal than those leaders who are simply making adjustments to an existing system. As discussed in chapter 3, in addition to having a high tolerance for ambiguity and dissent, these leaders must have a deep commitment to remedy existing weaknesses in the system and the ability to lead and inspire others to the same depth of commitment. They must be able to lead such an endeavor successfully over the long term, despite potential setbacks and the significant work that will be required to make changes in the day-to-day strategies and processes of teachers, administrators, support staff, and the school as a whole. They also must be strong enough to stay the course while managing all of the very real requirements and responsibilities of state and federal laws.

Clearly, strong organizational leadership is central, but at the same time, leaders in RISC schools must empower the staff to take the reins in any number of areas—not simply relative to classroom learning, such as making changes in instruction or writing standards-based rubrics, but in districtwide areas as well, such as leading community meetings, making school board presentations, chairing assessment committees, and so on. Leadership must be a shared responsibility and not simply the province of one or two individuals. If the model's success rests solely on the shoulders of one or two strong organizational leaders, there will be an insufficient foundation upon which to sustain the momentum of the change. If one or both of those leaders leaves the district, any improvements realized will likely be lost. Further, the quality and strength of relationships and organizational leadership matter greatly. Those schools and districts with the strongest ownership and leadership from teachers and administrators have come the farthest; conversely, those with significant turnover, or where commitment has been weak, have faltered.

Adopt High-Quality Standards-Based Grading and Reporting Software

In a standards-based system, teachers track the specific local or state standards covered by individual assignments, projects, and tests; evaluate students' progress in meeting these standards (via grades or rubric scores); and prepare report cards or provide information for student report cards about students' progress in meeting specific standards. Fortunately, as noted in chapter 3, grading and reporting software programs are available to help streamline, enhance, and centralize this process. Figure 4.3 is a screenshot from E-ducate software (www.3shapes.com) that shows how such software can be used to track students' progress.

This screenshot shows how a district or school can display a student's progress in relationship to the content areas and levels required for graduation. In this example, students must demonstrate proficiency at Level 6 in all of the required standards areas; and Level 7 standards are available in some content areas for students who are ready to pursue advanced content.

This screenshot also shows the student's average achievement for those standards levels that the student has completed, the number of required standards for the student has mastered in content areas the student is currently studying, and the student's average achievement level in standards areas not completed.

For example, in mathematics:

- The student's average demonstrated performance at Level 1 was advanced; Level 2, advanced; and Level 3, proficient.

- The student has completed 21 of 43 standards at Level 4. His or her average achievement for these 21 standards is "D" for "developing," using the four-point rubric of emerging, developing, proficient, advanced.

A high-quality software program can help teachers in a RISC school do the following:

- Create individual student report cards.

- Create individual standards-based transcripts.

- Identify areas of highest need—in terms of standards yet to master—for any student or group of students.

- Use rubrics to record students' progress in mastering any standards developmental level.

- Record comments about students' progress.

Figure 4.3: Sample Screenshot. Tracking Student Progress

Content Areas	Levels						
	01	02	03	04	05	06	07
CAREER AND CONTENT LITERACY	Proficient	Proficient	9 of 10 P				
COMMUNICATION	Proficient	Proficient	Proficient	2 of 16 D			
MATH	Advanced	Advanced	Proficient	21 of 43 D			
PERSONAL/SOCIAL/SERVICE SKILLS	Proficient	Proficient	Proficient				
READING	Proficient	Proficient	Advanced	3 of 11 D			
SCIENCE	Proficient	Proficient	Proficient	17 of 25 P			
SOCIAL STUDIES	Proficient	Proficient	13 of 15 P				
TECHNOLOGY	Proficient	Advanced	7 of 8 P				

Source: Provided by ThreeShapes LLC. For more information, see www.3shapes.com.

- Determine how groups of students are distributed across the developmental levels in any standards area.

- Analyze each student's progress toward completion of a developmental level—an invaluable instructional planning aid that helps ensure that instruction is based on student need.

The best software system allows students, teachers, and parents alike to access information about students' progress in mastering the developmental levels for each required standards area. Systems that track entries by date also encourage the timely entry of information about students' performance. Such a system encourages systemwide shared accountability and responsibility. Teachers must enter students' scores and comments about performance, but students, too, are responsible—in age- and maturity-appropriate ways—for knowing which levels they have mastered and which they have not, what content they need to learn next, and so on. They also are increasingly responsible for taking the initiative to move ahead in particular standards areas. The ability for students and teachers, as well as other stakeholders, to interface with the reporting and tracking system not only encourages responsibility, but reinforces the shared aspect of the RISC model: We are all in this together.

Develop a Community of Professionals With a Learner Mindset

Educators in RISC schools and districts are called on to do more than learn new grading, tracking, and reporting procedures. In fact, teachers who join a district using the RISC model go through a transformational process in terms of what it means to be an educator. In order to teach effectively in a system that is completely based on standards, most teachers must unlearn some of what they learned in their teacher preparation programs and let go of processes and practices that may have become habitual over the years, such as teaching straight from the textbook or using only forced-choice test items. Most experienced teachers know that there are better ways to teach, but it takes courage and energy to abandon long-used practices and learn new approaches, particularly when the school culture has not encouraged innovation in the past.

One key to ensuring success as teachers move through this process is ongoing professional development and collaboration. To provide teachers with opportunities to innovate, learn, and grow, school systems might offer content-area mentoring, support from other teachers and teacher-leaders, and focused professional development opportunities that are linked to school and individual teacher goals. The use of peer, supervisor, and self-evaluations is another strategy that fosters a culture of shared learning, ownership, and accountability at all levels. We recommend that teachers and administrators in a school system collaborate to create a standards-based teacher evaluation tool that follows the same continuum of mastery used to judge student performance (emerging, developing, proficient, and advanced).

A customized teacher evaluation tool, in place of the generic evaluation tool in use in many districts, speaks directly to the elements of the RISC model and can incorporate specific strategies for and expectations of teachers. Like students, teachers should be encouraged to change their perspectives of *success* and *failure*. A great deal of training and preparation is necessary to ensure that teachers understand the standards students must master, know how to write standards-based lesson plans, use standards-based classroom assessments and new grading processes, and gain a high degree of competence and facility in other aspects of a RISC environment. Being rated as *emerging* or *developing* on certain professional skills or areas of understanding, for example, does not equate to failure, particularly when growth and development are apparent. This perspective reinforces the systemwide cultural shift from one of isolated lone rangers working in separate classrooms to an interconnected body of professionals. When the school itself is a culture of learning for *all*, not simply for students, teachers find it easier to grant themselves permission to make mistakes, to learn from them, and to move on.

The need to unlearn past behaviors illustrates the difficulty inherent in the change process, regardless of a particular individual's intention and commitment. What teachers may struggle with, despite their commitment to a new education model, is the "reculturing" of the education system they knew, which Fullan (2001) describes as "transforming the culture—changing the way we do things around here" (p. 44).

Part of reculturing, Fullan asserts, is being off balance. However, when teachers stumble, they need support to get back on track. A natural reaction when a teacher tries something that does not work as well as he or she had hoped is to think, "I'm not going to make that mistake again" and take the safer, and likely less creative route next time. To support teachers in their own professional learning, RISC schools must shift the culture to one in which teachers have permission to fail—to make mistakes without punitive consequences; to stumble, pick themselves up, dust themselves off, and get right back to the business of educating children in a standards-based system.

It is critical to be clear that there is significant room for so-called errors, but creating a culture of learning (a collaborative team of professionals with a learner mindset) nonetheless may be met with resistance, particularly when the shifts occurring seem to conflict with "the way we do things around here." Not all teachers are able or willing to make the changes necessary in a newly minted RISC school; teacher turnover, therefore, can become an issue.

How do RISC systems attend to this issue? Alaska's Bering Strait School District tackled the issue of teacher ownership and retention head-on. District leaders, recognizing that teachers as well as students need learning opportunities that are relevant and meaningful, fundamentally altered the district's approach to professional development. A conscious decision was made to create a new breed of teacher-leaders who would be critical to the successful replication of the RISC model and, therefore, critical to students' success.

The district's past approach to professional development resembled that of most schools and districts. Kim Johnson, coordinator of educational support, who directs the district's staff development program, had this to say:

> At the beginning of the year, someone asked, "What's the new program for this year?" Then the approach was, "Let's put the entire district staff in the gymnasium where no one can hear anyway. Let's bring in a speaker who no one knows and who talks to us without a microphone for three days about something that isn't relevant to most of the staff." Then we sent people to unrelated things throughout the remainder of the year and never asked them to share or connect it to their practice. That was staff development.

RISC's benchmark for staff development is 30 days a year of inservice, a number that greatly exceeds the number of professional development days most districts set aside. The Bering Strait School District surpasses this already high standard by scheduling 42 days of staff development each year. The commitment is that every one of these days is relevant, engaging, and aligned with the district's standards and goals.

In line with that commitment, the district moved to a week-long conference that starts and ends with a keynote and offers sessions designed to appeal to a variety of audiences. A high school vocational teacher, for example, can find as many relevant sessions as a third-grade teacher, says Kim. The district also brings in individuals from other districts who are successfully doing what Bering Strait district leaders are trying to do.

In addition, instead of sending staff "willy-nilly per request and funding" without any accountability, says Kim, the district now requires staff members to tie what they hope to learn to one or more of the district's goals. In addition, when teachers return from a conference or workshop, they must complete a form that specifies how, when, and where they will share what they learned at the school and district level.

District surveys conducted since the launch of the new approach to staff development show that instead of resisting these changes, staff now perceive professional development as relevant, engaging, and enjoyable. The district is developing an online survey through which staff can address any specific component of the inservice—from the math content of a session to the quality of the accommodations—and make requests for specific presenters or topics.

These kinds of changes can act as a firewall against teacher turnover. In fact, RISC sites have experienced noteworthy decreases in teacher turnover, as much as 50%.

Prepare for the Changing Dynamics of Graduation

Graduation is a crucial topic in any school district. In a RISC school district, the topic of graduation is perhaps even more pivotal given the unique challenges and benefits of the RISC approach. Neither a standard high school diploma nor the equivalent credential (such as a GED certificate) matches the rigor of a diploma from a RISC school or district. To reiterate what has been said many times in this book, students in a RISC system must demonstrate—through standards-based assessments—that they truly grasp the knowledge or skill at each level. Students who demonstrate minimal understanding or competency will not simply be passed along.

The power and challenge of a RISC system is that students are granted the flexibility to move at their own pace in meeting this higher bar of learning. In practical terms, this means that the number of students graduating with their age peers will be smaller than expected in a traditional system. Some students will meet graduation requirements early—ahead of their age peers and earlier than what is expected or possible in traditional K–12 systems—perhaps as early as the first or second year of high school. Other students will need additional time beyond the traditional 4 years that typically encompass grades 9 through 12.

District teams should consider a variety of processes and programs to address the changing graduation landscape, including additional support structures (such as mentoring, advisory classes, and tutoring), more individualized instruction in multi-age classrooms, and Advanced Placement and other post-high school course offerings. Equally important is a shift in mindset that classes at any level will include students of a variety of ages.

The RISC model's flexible approach means that district leaders need to think and plan differently not only for students who need more time, but for those who advance at a quicker clip. Indeed, a lesson learned from the experiences of districts gearing up to the RISC approach is to begin to think of the 13 years of schooling, kindergarten through grade 12, as K–16, rather than K–12. The questions relative to students who meet graduation requirements early become, "What now? What's next for a graduating sophomore or junior?" Some of these students will choose to leave high school and immediately pursue a career or higher education options. Others, however, may choose to stay in the high-school setting. One option for these students is higher level course work, which may mean partnering with institutions of higher education, not only to determine course content but to offer college credit.

The initial years of RISC implementation will perhaps be the most challenging in terms of graduation, particularly the first year that district policy makes it clear that diploma granting will hinge on students demonstrating proficient or better performance on graduation-level assessments in each of the district's standards areas. Some students may not graduate with their classmates—even though up until this point they have been pushed along, year to year—and may spend an additional year or more mastering all of the levels required for high school graduation. This will be a very different outcome compared to the system these older students have become accustomed to in which a D or D– was enough to receive a diploma, regardless of what they actually learned.

When school systems first adopt the RISC model, older students may have an especially hard time with the dramatically different approach. They may resist completing the extra work needed to meet the new, higher academic bar. So-called fifth-year seniors may find it demoralizing to be held back rather than graduate with their peers, and there is some danger that students will drop out rather than do the hard work of meeting graduation-level requirements.

One very positive trend that has emerged from RISC district experiences is the number of dropouts who have returned to finish high school and graduate. A high percentage of RISC students who initially dropped out are returning to complete high school, whether it is a testament to the strength of a district's relationship with students, district leaders' unwavering commitment to hold the line, parent support for the RISC approach, or dropouts' wake-up call about the knowledge and skills needed to succeed in the world. Students' perception of how welcome they are in the high-school setting may also be a contributing factor. One notable policy instituted by Alaska's Bering Strait School District is to waive any additional fees the district could charge for returning students beyond the compulsory age of attendance. Explains Greg Johnson, director of curriculum and instruction, "We could charge them for attending, but instead our board and our superintendent have said, 'No, you are still our students. Come back and work with us.'"

High percentages of returning dropouts are by no means generally the case nationwide. An analysis by the National Center for Education Statistics

(2004) relative to the later educational attainment of a 1988 cohort of eighth graders offers interesting data relative to the future education pathways of dropouts. Of this cohort, 21% dropped out of high school at least once between eighth grade and 1994, 2 years after the time they would have graduated if they had completed school with their age peers. Of this group of dropouts, analysts found that just 19% had earned a high school diploma by 2000. An additional 44% had earned a high school equivalency credential, such as a GED (National Center for Education Statistics, 2004).

Like some students, parents also may be upset or unsettled at changing requirements. One of the toughest things for parents to deal with is when their children do not graduate with peers their age. Parents ask, "How can my child go to school for 12 or 13 years and not graduate? Students in our community who have been in school that long always have before."

Although some parents will likely be upset if their child is held back, others will view the situation as a positive compared to the past, particularly in communities where expectations run especially high. A hard look at graduates shows that students who were high school valedictorians or salutatorians can end up taking remedial courses when they go to college. It can be difficult for everyone—students, parents, and community members—to reconcile the notion that their "best and brightest" have not been adequately prepared to meet the expectations of post-secondary institutions.

By the same token, it may be clear that the existing system has not worked well for very-low-performing high school graduates either. Students who are pushed through, squeaking by with little deep core knowledge, might find themselves with a high school diploma in their back pocket but unable to do well enough on post-high school exams.

Although overall response from family members and the wider community in RISC systems has been quite positive, the mindset of A–F grades and end-of-the-year progress to the next year is so strong that the new approach continues to jar perspectives and well-ingrained frames of mind. Again, we come back to the notion of commitment. Schools and districts implementing the RISC model must have a strong commitment to stay the course for the longer range benefits students are sure to reap. Without such a grounded vision and purpose, it is all too easy to scrap the model and go back to the drawing board when the going gets tough. Administrators and board members need to hold strong to their position that students must demonstrate proficient or better performance in required standards areas in order to graduate—not just because it is policy, but because they believe it is the right thing to do for current students and for generations of students to come.

Begin the Continuous Improvement Process Early On

As discussed in chapter 3, continuous improvement and the RISC approach are nearly synonymous. The maxim "grow or die" captures the idea that failing to revisit, question, and renew—which includes abandoning unworkable practices, trying out promising strategies, and always reaching for what is next—sows the seeds for failure. A school or district that takes on the RISC approach must be one that welcomes change, not for the sake of change but for a vision of creating a better and better educational experience for students. This attitude toward change is visibly realized through the continuous improvement process, which should begin as soon as the RISC Approach to Schooling is up and running in the school or district, even at a few grade levels or only in core content areas.

Tools for continuous improvement are built into every aspect of a RISC system and are continually refined and strengthened. Similarly, in a RISC system stakeholders recognize that they are never "done"—there is always room for improvement, and taking this approach is in the best interests of their students.

The great value of clear, continuous improvement tools, used *across* the system, is that taking time to evaluate and correct is prioritized. As educators, we typically plan and do, but rarely, if ever, take time to evaluate what we have done or make refinements. By instilling a shared commitment to the process of continuous improvement, we give permission and mandate time to evaluate what we are doing for effectiveness and success.

To assist staff and school leaders as their systems move through the stages of change, the schools and districts that make up the Re-Inventing Schools Coalition developed the Organizational Self-Assessment Tool, or OSAT. This tool helps schools and districts analyze the extent to which their current practices are aligned with the four components of the RISC model: standards-based design, shared vision, leadership, and continuous improvement. As Figures 4.4 (page 149) and 4.5 (page 150) show, the OSAT includes descriptions of levels of change for more concrete aspects of the RISC model, such as assessments, as well as aspects of implementation that relate more closely to the skills and attributes of the individuals in the system, such as the extent to which leaders are adept at dealing with change. (See the appendix on page 177 for the complete OSAT.)

A school or district engaged in adopting the RISC model can use the OSAT to systematically check deployment of its school change plan and the organization's relative strength in each of the components of the RISC model. Once an organization has determined its current level of implementation, action steps can be identified that address the criteria of the next level(s).

The tool also can be used in a more refined manner to evaluate and plan progress. For instance, in the area of assessment, a district may determine that staff members are aware of the value of aligning instruction and internal assessments with local and state standards, that the district has a plan for developing internal assessments, and that some teachers are using standards-based assessments. However, by studying the OSAT descriptors, district leaders may realize that the district is lacking a *systematic* approach to assessing students' competence in all content areas, that teachers are using standards-based assessments but that they are not using them routinely, and that no process is in place for determining inter-rater reliability on internally developed assessments.

These observations can help the district set a specific course of action for strengthening its approach to assessment over time. As the culture of the district shifts, as supporting policies and processes are developed, as mindsets change, and as staff competence deepens, valid and reliable aligned assessments will systematically be used by all teachers to assess students' knowledge and skill. Eventually the district's assessments will be so strong that they will become benchmarks for other organizations.

Figure 4.4: Organizational Self-Assessment Tool. Assessment: Development and Deployment

Awareness	Understanding	First Implementation	Routine Use	Refinement	Replication
The organization is aware of the need to create standards-based internal assessments aligned to local standards and state assessment expectations and is willing to provide professional development on the use of standards-based assessment types (such as skills, analytical, self, and peer assessments).	The organization has developed a plan to create and implement internal assessments with supporting procedures and policies to systematize student progress through all content-area levels. The organization is beginning to use standards-based assessments.	The organization has developed at least one assessment type for each content-area level. Systematized processes and procedures are in place to advance students. Principals, teachers, and students demonstrate understanding and use the assessment processes and procedures.	The organization demonstrates systematic use of internal standards-based assessment types to assess mastery in all content-area levels. Assessment activities begin to involve parents. Data collection begins on inter-rater reliability. Plans and procedures are in place to review and refine assessments.	The organization's assessments are reviewed, edited, and revised at least twice on a regular cycle, and student performance indicates a high degree of predict-ability for success on external assessments. Assessment activities involve parents and community members in formally assessing student performance.	Organizational assessment, development, and implementation processes serve as a benchmark for others.

Source: Re-Inventing Schools Coalition. (2007). *Organizational Self-Assessment Tool.* Wasilla, AK: Author.

Figure 4.5: Organizational Self-Assessment Tool. Leadership. Change Adept

Awareness	Understanding	First Implementation	Routine Use	Refinement	Replication
The organization recognizes its role and responsibility to create healthy working environments through clear expectations, collaboration, effective communication, and promotion of healthy relationships.	The organization accepts responsibility for results and researches new opportunities for becoming a high-performing system. The organization works to increase stakeholder understanding of change theory.	The organization embraces the change process and promotes from their values and beliefs new innovations that inspire lively discussions about high-performing systems.	The organization initiates new ideas that are goal-oriented and systemic in nature. Leaders are willing to accept some dissent and ambiguity to improve the organization.	Organizational innovations lead to refinement of tools, policies, processes, and systematic deployment of ongoing improvement strategies to increase results. New paradigms are possible and encouraged.	Results from years of continued systemic improvement that have yielded clear processes are available for other organizations.

Source: Re-Inventing Schools Coalition. (2007). *Organizational Self-Assessment Tool.* Wasilla, AK: Author.

Results of RISC Replication

Efforts to replicate the RISC Approach to Schooling confirm that the replication process is challenging but has resulted in noteworthy improvements in the adopting systems. Among the results realized are the following:

- Significant, sustained increases in student achievement

- Increases in the number of students applying to, attending, and remaining in college

- Decreases in staff turnover

- Preliminary dips in senior graduation rates and increases in the number of fifth-year seniors, followed by increasing graduation rates and lower numbers of fifth-year seniors

- Significantly higher percentages of students passing high-stakes state assessments

In addition to these indicators of progress, overall results of RISC implementation are encouraging, as evidenced by the results of two key evaluations.

The first evaluation of the model's efficacy was initiated in 2005 when RISC contracted with researchers Gary Whiteley from Alaska and Theodore Coladarci and Lori Smith from the University of Maine to review the RISC Implementation Monitoring (RIM) Survey to ensure that survey items would result in statistically valid results. The RIM Survey is an electronic, web-based, self-assessment tool, aligned with the criteria articulated in RISC's Organizational Self-Assessment Tool (OSAT), developed to provide a roadmap for moving through the six levels of the RISC Change Continuum. (See earlier sections in this chapter for a discussion of the OSAT and the RISC Change Continuum.) Students, teachers, parents, and community members are surveyed, and the results are correlated with student achievement scores. RIM survey items focus on the extent to which a specific aspect of the model is being implemented. The survey is continually refined and fine-tuned to reflect stakeholder input while ensuring continued validity and reliability.

Coladarci, Smith, and Whiteley (2005) subsequently examined the relationship between student achievement and perceptions of RISC district respondents' regarding their level of implementation of the RISC model. The results of their study found that as respondents' perceptions increased, so, too, did the district's proficiency percentage in reading, writing, and mathematics.

In early 2005, employees in 16 Alaska school districts that were members of the Re-Inventing Schools Coalition participated in an online survey regarding their implementation of the model with respect to the four defining areas of the model: standards-based design, shared vision, leadership, and continuous improvement. Each district also provided student achievement data in reading, writing, and mathematics from Alaska's state-level exams for grades 3, 6, 8, and 10 for a 4-year period covering 2000–2001 through 2003–2004. These data included the percentage of students who had passed Alaska's state-level exams by scoring at the proficient or advanced level of performance. Coladarci et al. aggregated these data across grades to obtain one proficiency percentage for each district in each content area for each year.

Strong, positive correlations between respondents' perceptions of the districts' implementation of the model and the percentage of students who had passed Alaska's state-level exams were found for all three content areas assessed on the exam: reading, writing, and mathematics (.57, .33, and .54, respectively). Higher achievement was found in districts in which respondents reported higher levels of implementation, and lower achievement was found where lower levels of implementation were reported. In short, the higher the level of RISC implementation, the higher the level of student achievement.

A second, related study conducted by RISC analysts involved comparisons between five school districts in Alaska that were members of the Re-Inventing Schools Coalition and were implementing the model (Chugach School District, Lake and Peninsula School District, Mat-Su Umbrella Schools, Nome Public Schools, Northwest Arctic Borough School District) and five similar districts in Alaska that were *not* members of the coalition and *not* implementing the model (Chatham School District,

Dillingham City School District, Southwest Region School District, Yupiit School District, and Anchorage Alternative Schools: SAVE, Avail, Benson). Coalition school districts were chosen at random. Noncoalition districts were chosen based on the degree to which they were similar to the selected RISC districts based on area, student enrollment, the number of schools in the district, and the ethnicity of the student population.

Student achievement data for the 4-year period spanning 2000–2001 to 2003–2004 were aggregated to the district level and then to the coalition level, resulting in proficiency percentages for grades 3, 6, 8, and 10 in reading, writing, and mathematics. Figures 4.6, 4.7, and 4.8 (pages 153 and 154) show these results—in reading, writing, and math, respectively—for the five RISC districts or schools and the five similar noncoalition districts or schools. Figure 4.9 (page 155) reports the growth or loss in the percentage of students who scored at the proficient or advanced level across the 4 years, 2000–2001 through 2003–2004, in coalition versus noncoalition sites.

Figure 4.6: Coalition and Noncoalition Comparable Districts— Percentage of Students Proficient or Advanced in Reading from Aggregate Alaska Exam Data*

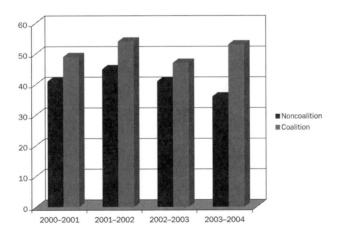

Source: Data used to create this figure are from "RISC vs. Similar Districts" (unpublished report) by the Re-Inventing Schools Coalition (October, 2005).

*Aggregate of student achievement results at grades 3, 6, 8, and 10 on Alaska's required state-level exams.

Figure 4.7: Coalition and Noncoalition Comparable Districts—Percentage of Students Proficient or Advanced in Writing From Aggregate Alaska Exam Data*

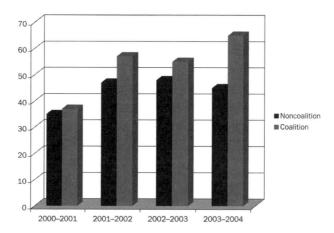

Source: Data used to create this figure are from "RISC vs. Similar Districts" (unpublished report) by the Re-Inventing Schools Coalition (October, 2005).

*Aggregate of student achievement results at grades 3, 6, 8, and 10 on Alaska's required state-level exams

Figure 4.8: Coalition and Noncoalition Comparable Districts—Percentage of Students Proficient or Advanced in Math From Aggregate Alaska Exam Data*

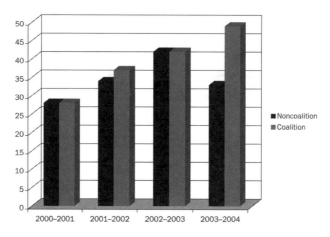

Source: Data used to create this figure is from "RISC vs. Similar Districts" (unpublished report) by the Re-Inventing Schools Coalition (October, 2005).

*Aggregate of student achievement results at grades 3, 6, 8, and 10 on Alaska's required state-level exams

Figure 4.9: Coalition and Noncoalition Comparable Districts—Change in Percentage of Students Proficient or Advanced From Alaska Exams* 2000–2001 to 2003–2004

	Reading	Writing	Math	Total Growth, 4 Years	Average Growth, 4 Years
Coalition	4.26%	27.34%	20.94%	52.54%	17.51%
Noncoalition	–5.27%	9.44%	5.59%	9.76%	3.25%

Source: Data from "RISC vs. Similar Districts" (unpublished report) by the Re-Inventing Schools Coalition (October, 2005).

*Alaska Benchmark exams and Alaska High School Graduation Qualifying Exams

Taking Action

The first step in implementing a truly standards-based system is the recognition that, whatever your role—whether you are a teacher, principal, superintendent, school board member, or policymaker—there are things you can do to start the replication ball rolling.

If You Are a Teacher

- Try out some of the processes discussed in this book.

- Visit RISC online at www.reinventingschools.org. Learn as much as you can about RISC's work.

- Visit a school or classroom that practices the RISC philosophy.

- Ask yourself these questions:

  ▸ Do my students know what they must accomplish to move to the next level? Is it clear to them what they need to learn? Can they explain that to someone else?

  ▸ Are there clear roadmaps in my classroom that explain levels of proficiency?

  ▸ What will students learn this year? And how is that content being scaffolded?

  ▸ Do I collaborate with teachers of different grade levels to ensure that our curriculum is taught consistently and efficiently?

▸ Does learning occur when I am not in the room? Are students engaged after school hours?

If You Are a Principal

- Compare your school's practices with the practices identified in RISC's Organizational Self-Assesessment Tool.

- Create a 2-minute classroom checkup to determine whether standards are being learned, how they are being assessed, and how that information is being reported back to students and parents.

- Determine whether your school's teacher evaluation tool aligns with the RISC model and best practices.

- Ask yourself these questions:

  ▸ What does a traditional high-quality classroom look like?

  ▸ What does a standards-based classroom look like?

  ▸ How do I know that my school has clear targets, assessments, and reporting documents tied to standards?

  ▸ How does our teacher-evaluation process reflect our goals?

  ▸ Does our evaluation tool align with the RISC model and best practices? More specifically, are teachers soliciting ideas from students about what they want the culture of the classroom to be like, how conflicts will be resolved, and how students will treat one another? Are students engaged in learning? Are teachers using a high-quality continuous improvement process, such as RISC's VISA process or another strong PDSA cycle?

If You Are a Superintendent

- Begin to design a school or district that is standards based.

- Convene a cross-district team to discuss the RISC Approach to Schooling, current district policies and practices that support learning, and ingrained, unproductive habits.

- Ask yourself these questions:

- ▶ What are our standard operating procedures for ensuring quality in our classrooms, in our schools, and across the district?

- ▶ How does our district compare with similar districts and with districts of higher socioeconomic status in terms of student achievement, teacher retention, and other indicators of high-performing organizations?

- ▶ What are the steps necessary to become a world-class district?

- ▶ How can we be sure to hire the right people and then support them and help them develop as professionals?

If You Are a School Board Member

- Share this book with your constituents: administrators, parents, teachers, and your fellow board members.

- Once a new direction is in place, hire the right superintendent who has the desire, skills, and mindset to deploy this system.

- Adopt board policy that commits to moving from a traditional time-based, credit-driven system to a standards- and performance-based system.

- Ask yourself these questions:

  - ▶ Do we have a vision that everyone shares and can articulate?

  - ▶ Does our current system educate all students in a way that will enable them to become economically self-sufficient?

  - ▶ What does it mean to be world class?

  - ▶ How can I help shape board policy to support this journey?

If You Are a Policymaker

- Become familiar with your current education policies, and examine them for equity and quality.

- Understand what it means to create a world-class system and what the key components of such a system are.

- Learn about the Malcolm Baldrige National Quality Award (www. baldrige.nist.gov) and the Baldrige Education Criteria for Performance Excellence (www.quality.nist.gov/Education_Criteria.htm).

- Ask yourself these questions:

  ▶ What does it mean to ensure equity and quality in our schools?

  ▶ What are the kinds of policies we need to build world-class systems?

  ▶ How can I support innovations and new systems that are about being world class?

  ▶ How can we attract and retain the best and brightest to teach and lead in our schools?

  ▶ What are other countries doing that we should study?

5

Student Stories:
Individual Lives and
Futures Transformed

Leading Questions

1. How many of your students are engaged in their education?

2. Can students articulate your education system and their place in it? For example, can they explain the vision of the system and how their learning goals relate to that vision, as well as what they are learning and why?

3. What are students doing after they leave your system? For example, are they pursuing trade school, secondary education, entrepreneurial activities, or jobs in the workplace?

The RISC Approach to Schooling has affected the lives of hundreds of students in Alaska and a growing number in the Lower 48 states. This chapter highlights the stories of two very different Alaskan students, from rural Tatitlek and urban Anchorage, respectively.

Rami's Story, Tatitlek Community School

It is 6:15 a.m. in Tatitlek, Alaska, a remote Native village situated southeast of Anchorage on a tip of land between the Tatitlek Narrows and Boulder Bay in Alaska's Prince William Sound. The sun is not yet up in this small Alutiiq community, but Rami Totemoff, age 16, is.

Since 5:30 this morning, Rami has been focused on completing a project for school. It is one of a number of projects she must complete in the next several months if she hopes to graduate with her classmates. By 6:50, she is out the front door of her parents' home for the short walk around the bend and up the hill to school. Rami has been following this routine every weekday for the past 9 months, ever since she says she "woke up" and realized she might not graduate.

Rami was born in Tatitlek and has attended the same school since she was old enough to go to school—Tatitlek Community School, which sits at the top of a gravel road overlooking the water. This K–12 school of some 30 students is part of the rural Chugach School District.

Tatitlek, Alutiiq for "land of the wind," is a 7.3-square-mile spot of land accessible only by plane or boat. Visitors from Anchorage, Alaska's urban hub, typically arrive via a 40-minute ride on an eight-seat Navajo or other bush plane. Like other Native villages throughout Alaska, Tatitlek has no malls, no coffee shops, no movie theaters, and no fast food drive-thrus. It also has no grocery store or gas station of any kind. It does have two small churches, a community center, Tatitlek Community School, the quiet beauty of the waters of Prince William Sound against the backdrop of Copper Mountain, and unbroken 180-degree views of the Chugach Mountain Range. The 110 or so residents of Tatitlek have a subsistence lifestyle or earn their living from fish processing and oyster farming.

For many years, teachers at Tatitlek Community School, like teachers in most U.S. schools, followed a traditional approach to schooling. They delivered "one size fits all" lessons, administered standardized tests, handed out letter grades, and moved as many students as possible from grade level to grade level at the end of each academic year. As a young student, Rami was an extremely poor reader with learning disabilities. She was also bored and unmotivated to do anything with her life or education.

In 1994, Chugach School District administrators, motivated by a commitment to impact the district's startlingly poor statistics, moved into action and began to develop a fundamentally different approach to educating the district's students. The new philosophy meant that students would have opportunities to learn, grow, and succeed in ways they never had; it also meant, however, it would not be enough for students to simply sit back and do the minimum required, not if they hoped to graduate.

Rami's parents, Evelyn and Roy, were two of the district's biggest supporters right from the beginning. They attended communitywide meetings and potlucks with district administrators who flew from Anchorage to meet and talk with the community about the new approach and seek their ideas on the kinds of educational changes needed.

Evelyn and Roy spoke repeatedly with Rami about the importance of taking her schoolwork seriously, but Rami would not listen. Year after year, she sat in class, ignoring everyone's attempts to engage her in learning. The one thing she *was* interested in doing was chatting with her friends online.

Finally, when Rami was 16, her dad sat her down and gave her what he calls his "big speech." "You can sit here at your computer and talk to people all you want," he said, "and then you can go to work down here at the village oyster farm. Or you can go to school and see the world."

Something that her dad said finally clicked for Rami. With less than 9 months remaining before the time she always thought she would graduate, it was clear to her that she would not graduate if she kept doing what she had been doing. She realized that the district's philosophy of education meant that her teachers would not simply pass her along from year to year. She had to work for this diploma. When Rami "woke up," she was the equivalent of 3 years behind in her schooling. "I was in my third year of high school," she says, "but my academic level was about a freshman level."

Almost overnight, Rami became a new student. When she did, everyone got behind her—her parents, her teachers, family, and friends. The failing student with the bad attitude became motivated, engaged in learning, and determined to succeed. Over the next several months, Rami became almost single-mindedly focused on learning and graduating.

During this time, she studied and worked—at school, at home, before school, after school, and on weekends—and soaked up every opportunity to learn. Anchorage House, a district-developed residential learning program established in Alaska's largest urban community, provided numerous rich, extended learning opportunities beyond village life. For example, Rami was one of several students and adults who took a week-long camping/kayaking trip to Moab, Utah, where they traveled down an 85-mile-long river in a canoe, bought and prepared all the meals, and created various learning scenarios.

On May 28, 2005, Rami graduated with the other students in her class. "Everyone cried . . . my parents, my teachers, my friends," recalls Rami. "It was a great day."

The day after graduation, Rami flew to Fairbanks to attend the Rural Alaska Honors Institute, a transition program for high school Alaska Native honors students bound for college. After participating in the Institute in 2005, Rami began her first year as an undergraduate student in 2006 at the University of Alaska at Anchorage, thanks to five different scholarships. She subsequently decided to take time off from her university studies to complete an internship through the Chenega Corporation, one of the Alaska Native corporations created as a result of the Alaska Native Claims Settlement Act enacted by Congress in 1971. As part of her internship, she worked in Virginia and then in Cuba.

In August 2008, Rami enrolled in a year-long informational technology program at AVTEC (Alaska Vocational Technical Center), in Seward, Alaska. After completing the program, she plans to return to the University of Alaska to complete her degree and then work with the Chenega Corporation after graduation.

"If we still had the old system, I may have graduated from high school, but I wouldn't have learned anything," says Rami. "The Chugach School District helped me so much. They gave me so many opportunities. I am now an adult who can stand up and say, 'I'm a successful person and I'm going to be somebody.'"

Zach's Story, Highland Tech High

Zach Maurer was born in Anchorage and has lived there ever since. In 2002, Zach was preparing to begin middle school in Anchorage, at the same local school his older sister had attended, but he was nervous. His sister, who had always been a good student, started falling behind in high school. "I saw this traditional school chew my sister up and spit her out," says Zach. "I wasn't very social, and I was worried about that aspect of it. And as I walked through the hall during orientation, I got scared. I told my parents that this school wouldn't do it." Zach's parents took his concerns seriously, pulling him out of the public school system and homeschooling him for seventh grade.

But homeschooling, too, was not working for Zach. He struggled with the idea that his mother was his only teacher, and his home was the classroom. As seventh grade drew to a close, Zach began to look for other options. "This was right as Highland Tech High was opening," Zach recalls. "When I went to the orientation and walked through the hallways, it seemed like the place for me." Zach's parents fully supported Zach's desire to enroll at Highland Tech. They supported him and pushed him—in the right ways—to go farther, but they also taught him to do things on his own. Always a good, self-motivated student whose achievement was above average, Zach nonetheless found the transition—not only back to public schooling but to this new model of schooling—challenging but exciting at the same time.

Depending on the class, he might be in a room with a mixed age range or in a setting that more closely mirrored a traditional classroom, with students who were roughly the same age and grade level. In addition, depending on how the class was structured, teachers might teach in different ways. In Zach's math class, for example, the multi-age group of students worked at developmental levels ranging from level 3 to level 6. In Zach's Alaska Studies class, conversely, students were primarily 11th and 12th graders, working within a narrower range of developmental levels; as a result, there was more direct instruction. In Highland Tech High's first years, students worked on different topics (for example, statistics and probability, or functions and relationships) within the different standards levels, as teachers circulated throughout the room as needed. Teachers have since refined their approach, teaching the same topic within the same class period, albeit at a range of developmental levels.

Although Zach's initial weeks and months at Highland Tech were spent getting up to speed about the standards-based approach, as one of the first students through the school's newly opened doors, he found that everyone—students, teachers, and administrators—was in the same boat.

"One of the things that was great about being in the first wave of students at Highland Tech was that we were all learning together," Zach recalls.

"Our teachers didn't always have all of the answers. It was an adjustment to move to the standards-based approach, but we supported each other along the way. It was like one big family."

As Zach progressed through the developmental levels at Highland Tech High, he took on more and more leadership. The student who was worried about social life in a traditional school became involved in nearly every organization the school offered. In addition to participating in a robotics program, Zach served as editor of the school newspaper and coeditor of the yearbook. He also participated in the school's Principal Cabinet. By the time he took part in the Principal's Cabinet, he recalls, he had been at Highland Tech High for a few years, so he was accustomed to being empowered. "Even so," Zach says, "it was so great to be heard—to be able to tell my peers, their parents, and the principal what I thought, and to really be heard. It gave me a sense that I was truly involved with my school, that I could make a difference."

In 2007, Zach graduated a year early at age 17, and the valedictorian of his class. Shortly thereafter, he began his first year at the University of Alaska at Anchorage, where he is pursuing a full course load, including language studies in Japanese and French, as he gives more thought to his future career. He is considering three career pathways: corporate attorney, architect, or civil engineer. Given Zach's evident leadership, self-reflection, and maturity, it is clear that regardless of the path he chooses, he will indeed make his mark.

6

Hope for the Future: A Million Kids, a Thousand Districts

From the outside looking in, it can be easy to believe that small schools in Alaska's rural villages have little in common with schools in New York, Detroit, Houston, or Atlanta—or even equally small schools in the badlands of South Dakota. One of the criticisms RISC leaders have heard is that their efforts worked because the approach was initiated and replicated in Alaska—that somehow the dynamics of Alaska and the innate attributes of the individuals who live there conspired to create an environment in which deep reform has taken place that cannot take place anywhere else.

Alaskan folks may like to view themselves as unique pioneers, and in many ways they are, but what they did can be done by individuals in any school district in America. What happened for Rami Totemoff in rural Tatitlek and Zach Maurer in urban Anchorage can happen for any student in any community.

Despite the obvious differences in geography, climate, and cultural dynamics—differences that are no more dramatic than the differences between a school district in the Bronx and one in the Deep South—conditions in Alaska's school districts are similar to conditions in any school district across the country (rural, suburban, or urban; small, medium, or large). Even the best districts have students who struggle for any number of reasons—substance abuse, poverty, tumultuous family dynamics, or simply the challenges of growing up. Even the poorest school systems have gifted students who are not reaching their potential. In addition, pre-RISC Alaskan education systems and traditional education systems elsewhere look remarkably alike: an educational process driven by long-established policies and a culture resistant to change—a system that seems to have lost its way.

Conversations about what does not work in public education are not new, nor are potential solutions to address those problems. However, there is a new context, a new climate for the conversation. A blurring of economic borders, heightened awareness of the impact of a marketplace driven by innovations in technology, and clarity that some version of the No Child Left Behind Act is here to stay have created a new sense of urgency about the U.S. education system, nudging many more of us closer to the realization that some of the most fundamental aspects of the traditional education system need to be overhauled. In other words, there is a new opening to deliver on the promise of American education.

The seeds of what would become known as the RISC Approach to Schooling began with a single teacher, in a single classroom, trying to do what was best for a single group of students. When Rich DeLorenzo first began to study the research and try out new things in his classroom, he simply wanted to help kids learn. He likely could not have imagined where it would lead: to a revolution in the Chugach School District and to the creation of a coalition dedicated to refining Chugach's processes—and then replicating that approach worldwide in service to students.

The Re-Inventing Schools Coalition is casting the net wide to replicate, on a national level, what a few schools and districts are doing on a local level. The system can work, not just in Alaska, or in small schools, or in unusual settings, but in our largest, most diverse public school systems. It can be replicated, and given the right supports and commitment, it can be sustained. It is, at this juncture, the best chance we have of making real our collective commitment—still stubbornly unrealized—to every young person, of every color, socioeconomic status, background, or apparent ability to learn.

The Re-Inventing Schools Coalition is committed to replicating the RISC Approach to Schooling in at least 1,000 districts, reaching one million students, what RISC leaders call the "tipping point." Although they are the first to admit that they do not have all the answers, every day they take focused actions—in the present—to move toward that future.

The journey toward a RISC system begins with these questions: Are we really trying to create a world-class education system? If so, we need to dramatically change what we are doing. Do we really want to educate all kids? If so, we need to challenge some of the longest-standing aspects of traditional education—those "blind spots" that have limited our view of what is possible for each and every student.

Challenges, known and unknown, most certainly will arise along the road to reinvention. But as our actions mirror our commitments, a world-class system of education can emerge for all children. Much of the groundwork for this system has been laid by the scouts and trailblazers who are members of the Re-Inventing Schools Coalition.

The 1% Solution

You may have heard or read the story, relayed in Jack Canfield and Mark Hansen's book *Chicken Soup for the Soul* (1993), about the man who was walking on a beach in Mexico one day when he came across a local native who was picking up starfish from the sand and, one by one, throwing them back into the ocean. Apparently it was low tide and the starfish, if not soon returned to the waters, would die from lack of oxygen. The beach was strewn with thousands of starfish. When asked why he continued to work on such a seemingly impossible task, on one beach among hundreds of others like it, the native replied as he threw another starfish into the water, "Made a difference for that one!"

We do not know for certain, but we get the impression that the man who met the native on the beach was simply asking a question, "Why are you doing that?" Some critics of the RISC approach simply ask questions; others task the patience and goodwill of RISC's best, most fair-minded leaders.

Adopting the RISC approach means moving away from the comforts of textbooks, measuring student seat time, and other aspects of the traditional system of schooling. "It is very challenging for people to change these behaviors," says Rich DeLorenzo. "Just look at how hard it is for us to stay on a diet or change the way we exercise. To change a whole philosophy of education is a daunting undertaking."

For those readers who are thinking, "That's right. It can't be done. It will never happen in my school or district," you are right. If you do not think it can happen, it will not. But we have a choice: We can either have our excuses and reasons, or we can have the results we envision.

Top 10 Excuses to Guarantee No Change

1. We're satisfied with our results. Most of our students graduate, and many are very successful in life. What's the point in changing?

2. This is the way I was taught to teach. The university I attended was world-renowned, so they must know what's best.

3. School was good enough for me, so it should be good enough for my children.

4. My child is a high achiever, and the system is working fine for her. Let's not rock the boat. Besides, this only applies to students at the low end.

5. Our district doesn't have leaders who are willing to commit to changing the system.

6. Our district is different. Besides, we are already using standards.

7. We're too small/We're too big.

8. We tried something like that once before.

9. We don't have the money.

10. It sounds like a lot of work.

What kind of person acknowledges excuses and reasons, but puts them aside to stand for something higher? What kind of person is willing to challenge a system that is so well-established in every sense—culturally, financially, and even emotionally? What kind of individual is willing to be the one to lead a group in an entirely new direction? What kind of person throws starfish after starfish back into the ocean?

Maybe it is the 1% in any audience who will take on the challenge—the 1% we can't wait to meet. Within this 1% are people who may be uncomfortable with change, but are not stopped by change, people who embrace problems, people who recognize but are not dissuaded by the dissenters in the crowd. These people—the critical 1% solution—can dramatically impact the future of education everywhere. They have the choice, as Rich states it, to "do what's easy or do what's right."

Over the course of the journey described in this book, that 1% has had the courage to confront the brutal facts and tell the truth about their students and their school systems. Individual parents have stood beside district leaders in the toughest times. Board members have stepped out and spoken up about the promise of this approach, despite criticism and reproach from colleagues.

Rebecca Midles is one example of the individuals who make up the 1% solution. Inspired by her parents, both of whom she describes as "incredible educators who were always doing things differently," Rebecca initially had decided to go into politics to try to change the education system as a policymaker. But in 1998, she attended a job fair where there were lines out the door wherever Rich DeLorenzo and Roger Sampson spoke on behalf of the Chugach School District.

Rich and Roger's policy at the time was not to accept applications from anyone until they had listened to the district's presentation. "Most people would leave," Rich recalls, "when they saw that we were challenging the system and that we were going to do things differently." Rebecca was one person who stayed. As she listened to Rich speak that day, she decided to forego her plans to go into politics and become a teacher first. "I realized," Rebecca says, "how much more meaningful it would be to be an elected official some day who had actually been a teacher. When I heard Rich say that they had found a better way to educate kids, that it could be different, I couldn't wait to get involved."

At the time, Rebecca did not have her teaching certification, so she did not apply for a position with the Chugach School District. She was frustrated because she thought she was "too late to the game," but everything Rich talked about that day was never far from her thoughts. In 2000, 2 years after she heard that presentation, Rebecca graduated with a master's degree in education and her teaching certificate. It was not long before she was teaching in a standards- and project-based environment. Today, Rebecca is the assistant principal, director of curriculum, and an English teacher at Highland Tech High, influencing the lives of hundreds of students.

The Leading Edge of Uncertainty

The RISC Approach to Schooling, and the specific ways in which it plays out day to day in real classrooms, with real teachers, with real students, is constantly evolving. This ongoing evolution is a natural, positive outgrowth of the shared commitment RISC leaders have to ensure that the model makes a lasting difference for all students everywhere.

RISC leaders are the first to say that they do not have all the answers, and that the specifics of the RISC approach are not perfectly ironed out. Therein lies the model's weakness and strength—its weakness in that some step-by-step guidance is in place to make it happen, but not every detail is yet articulated; its strength is that enough guidance is in place to ensure replication. In other words, enough core principles and details have been clarified and enough mandates are missing to allow for the greatest local ownership of the model and the greatest benefit from a continuous improvement process that makes the specifics of the RISC approach somewhat of a moving target.

As schools and districts that have implemented the RISC approach reach higher levels of refinement and experience, they become models of what is possible in any school or district. The RISC team refers to these educational organizations as "lighthouses"—school sites that are beacons for those stakeholders considering taking on the challenge in their own organizations.

These lighthouse sites show that change on a systems level can be accomplished, as well as how it can be accomplished. As they share their results and show how changes in the teaching culture have occurred, how school-community partnerships can work, and how students, even very young ones, can be leaders in their educational process, the vision and the ideal become concrete and the potential for transforming each of the 17,000 school districts in America becomes a reality.

Every process and structure of the RISC approach may not be nailed down in concrete, sequential order, but what is assured is that RISC leaders are passionately working to bring into existence a new paradigm, a new future, for U.S. education. Those who are on the leading edge of this movement are in the field, applying the model, making adjustments, sharing what they have learned, and learning from setbacks. In other words, they are in a constant state of refinement and growth. They are on the leading edge of uncertainty, and they would not want to be anywhere else. They welcome feedback about the model as conceptualized here, but more important, they seek committed partners—both organizations that will become lighthouses as well as individuals who will think together and work together to create an even more effective system. In other words, they seek partners who will stand with them on the leading edge—at times, the bleeding edge—of uncertainty, yet one that is brimming with the immense possibility of delivering on the promise of education for every student.

Taking Further Action: What You Can Do

For those of you who are called to stand on the front line with RISC leaders, here are a few action steps we invite you to take.

1. *Learn More About the Re-Inventing Schools Coalition and the RISC Approach to Schooling*

Undertake a due diligence process about the Re-Inventing Schools Coalition. Visit RISC online at www.reinventingschools.org. The web site includes information about the RISC model, upcoming RISC events, consulting services, and links to resources. The site also provides access to a Wiki community—an online tool that allows many individuals to contribute and share resources, and collaborate with RISC schools and districts to codevelop standards-based tools and processes.

2. Talk With Us, Email Us, and Communicate With Us

The RISC team is happy to talk with you, answer questions, and help you get started. Contact them directly:

Rich DeLorenzo: rdelorenzo@gci.net

Wendy Battino: wbattino@reinventingschools.org

Rick Schreiber: rschreiber@reinventingschools.org

3. Attend a RISC Conference

Get involved. See www.reinventingschools.org for information about upcoming RISC conferences.

4. Talk With Your Congressperson

Start a conversation about the No Child Left Behind Act, about education, and about public education in the United States.

5. Begin to Implement Where You Have a Locus of Control

Chapter 4 includes numerous suggestions and guidance for superintendents, principals, policymakers, teachers, and school board members.

6. Call, Write, or Visit Schools and Districts That Are Deploying the RISC Approach to Schooling

See www.reinventingschools.org for the most recent list of RISC school sites.

7. Pay It Forward

Pass this book along to a friend, a colleague, your principal or superintendent, a board member, or a parent; buy two books and give one away. Write a note in the front of the second one: "I think this will make a difference in your life."

8. Become Passionate About Improving the Quality of Life for All People

I always advise teachers: The only true task at the end of the day is to go home and look yourself in the mirror and say, "What did I do today? What did I do for students?"

—Greg Johnson, Director of Curriculum and Instruction,
Bering Strait School District

The Quad Chairlift: A Chance Meeting

A number of years ago during RISC's annual winter institute, held each year at Alaska's Alyeska Resort, Rich was riding the quad chairlift with three Alaska Native boys whom he had never met and who had no idea who Rich was. He cannot recall their names, but for purposes of this story, we will call them Corey, Jason, and Mike.

As they rode the lift to the top of the mountain, Rich turned to the boys and said, "Hi guys! How are you doing? Where are you from?"

Corey responded, "We're from the Bering Strait School District."

"How's school?"

"We're trying something different there."

"Oh, really. What's that?"

"It's this thing called the RISC model."

"What's that all about?"

"We work at our own rate through different levels. It tries to help prepare us for the future."

"How's it working?"

"It's really good for me and my friend Jason."

"Why?"

"Because we're in 10th grade, and we know what we need to do to graduate."

"How about your friend here?"

"Mike? He's a senior. He doesn't have to do it."

"How's that make you feel, Mike?"

"I'm glad I'm graduating in a few months because I wouldn't like that system. I'd have to change everything I'm doing and be more accountable for learning."

"Is that a bad thing?"

"Well, yeah, because I'd have to work a lot harder. It's much easier to just work in the textbooks our teachers have used all these years."

Rich turned to Corey and Jason and asked, "What do you think?"

"We think what we're doing is better," said Jason, "because we're going to be better prepared than Mike is and we're going to have more choices in our lives."

By then they had reached the summit of the mountain. As Rich got off the chairlift, he turned to the boys and said, "That sounds like a good thing. You boys are lucky to be in that system. It's too bad more schools aren't like yours. Have a nice day, and be safe!"

As this story illustrates, the impact of the RISC philosophy on individual students' lives can be quite positive, but it requires students to take actions that may be uncomfortable or unfamiliar to them. For those students who take these actions, the results can be life-altering. Students who may not have graduated receive their diplomas; students who may have settled for low-skill, low-wage jobs move on to college and a brighter future. Students who were bored or frustrated in school find themselves pursuing career paths that are a match for their highest aspirations and dreams.

What makes us think achievement will rise in a system in which students move at their own pace and the academic bar is set high? The answer is quite simple: We will accept no less.

"I've been lucky as a student to take control of my learning and lucky as a person to understand myself. I realize the importance of *one*. If one teacher can change a classroom and *one* principal can change a school, then I know *one* student can change the world. All I have to do is try."

—Zach Maurer, Graduate,
Highland Tech High
Anchorage, Alaska

The philosophy underlying the RISC model grew into a system of schooling because of a single person who wanted to help his students, then two committed district leaders who inspired a group of educators who risked their careers, professional ridicule, and failure. A district may have one school or one teacher who says, "This is the right way to help kids learn." That is all we need. As that one school site or one individual teacher begins to change individual students' lives, the results will speak for themselves, and others will be clamoring for more.

Appendix A

RISC Organizational Self-Assessment Tool (OSAT)

This tool is for organizational assessment. It is divided into the four components of the RISC Approach to Schooling: Standards-Based Design, Shared Vision, Leadership, and Continuous Improvement. Standards-Based Design is further divided into four subcomponents: Standards, Instruction, Assessment, and Recording and Reporting, each of which is further divided into specific traits. As the RISC Approach to Schooling has evolved, we have found that using the phrase *recording and reporting*, in place of the phrase *grading and reporting*, better captures the unique RISC view of the seamless, transparent system of students participating in various assessments, teachers and others recording data about students' performance, and the system then reporting this rich body of information to students, parents, and other stakeholders.

The purpose of this tool is to guide reflection on your current practices aligned to the RISC Approach. Criteria in the tool are based on best practice and current research. To use the tool, simply underline the specific criteria along each continuum that best identify where you are as an organization. To identify the organizational working level for an entire component, identify the indicator in which all criteria for each trait are met. Used on a semi-annual basis, the tool can highlight progress made and assist in the development of objectives, action plans, and key performance indicators (KPIs).

Descriptions of each of the indicators:

Awareness: The organization is interested in pursuing or believes that there is a need for these practices and processes. Members of the organization may have discussed these ideas and may have done some initial research but have not approached the concepts in a formal way as an organization.

Understanding: The organization has begun researching and planning to formally address these practices and processes. The organization desires to increase the capacity of individuals who know how to do these processes and have begun to provide professional development opportunities for stakeholders.

First Implementation: The organization is working purposefully to formalize these practices and processes. The organization has detailed plans in place and has begun implementation, but has not completed sufficient steps to collect data on the success of implementation.

Routine Use: The organization regularly uses these practices and processes as part of routine throughout the organization. Members of the organization willingly and purposefully engage in these practices and processes. The organization has data spanning at least one cycle time showing positive growth.

Refinement: The organization has established cycle times and processes to continuously improve practices. The organization has reviewed and refined the practices and processes over two or more cycle times. The organization has data to demonstrate positive growth trends for 3 or more years.

Replication: The organization possesses the capacity and experience to assist other districts with these practices and processes. The organization has willingly made available to interested organizations examples of current practices and processes.

STANDARDS-BASED DESIGN

	Traits	Awareness	Understanding	First Implementation	Routine Use	Refinement	Replication
Overall	**Strategic Planning**	The organization is aware of and is interested in pursuing the development of district standards and implementation of a standards-based system aligned to the organization's focus areas.	The organization is developing a plan to implement a standards-based system (for example, local standards tied to focus areas, student placement and progress, assessments, reporting tools), Carnegie unit waiver is requested.	Organization policies, resources, and schedules are being aligned to the implementation of the standards-based system. Carnegie unit waiver is implemented with a transition plan for older students.	Organization policies, resources, and schedules are aligned to a standards-based system. Carnegie unit waiver is fully implemented.	Organization policies, resources, and schedules have been refined at least twice on a regular cycle, are aligned to a standards-based system, and the transition plan is completed.	Organizational plans and policies associated with the standards-based system serve as a benchmark for other organizations.
Standards	**Input**	The organization sees value in including stakeholder input to develop local standards and researching a variety of district, state, and national standards for content, format, and best practices.	Organizational activities (for example, strategic planning, community meetings, and standards committees) clearly support the inclusion of teacher, community, parent, student, and business input regarding local standards.	Organizational activities foster student/parent ownership and understanding of standards. Stakeholders can explain the use of standards and identify differences from a traditional system.	Organizational activities advance student ownership, responsibility, and participation in standards-based processes (for example, personal learning plans [PLPs], student tracking sheets, portfolios, and student-led parent conferences).	The organization has implemented formal processes to give parents, community, students, staff, and businesses opportunities for additional input on standards and related processes.	Stakeholder familiarity with the processes allows them to assist other organizations in developing practices for creating stakeholder ownership.

STANDARDS-BASED DESIGN

	Traits	Awareness	Understanding	First Implementation	Routine Use	Refinement	Replication
Standards	Development and Deployment	The organization is aware of state standards and grade-level equivalencies, and understands the need to support the development of local standards through professional development.	The organization is actively pursuing the development of local standards that incorporate stakeholder input and are aligned to state standards. Standards clearly indicate what stakeholders believe students need to know and be able to do.	The organization has developed, and made accessible to all stakeholders, local standards in traditional and non-traditional content-area levels. Students are placed in developmentally appropriate content-area levels.	The organization has edited, revised, and aligned standards to internal and external indicators of student success.	The organization's standards and resources are reviewed, edited, and revised at least twice on a regular cycle, and student performance indicates high degree of predictability for success on external assessments.	District standards and resources serve as a benchmark for other organizations.
Instruction	Standards and Assessment	The organization believes that an established set of local standards should drive instruction.	The organization documents the expectation that standards will drive instruction. All classroom planning, instruction, and assessments are standards-referenced and begin to show standards-based practices aligned to local standards.	The organization implements procedures and policies (for example, lesson planning, student progress through content-area levels, teacher/principal evaluation tools, and recording and reporting procedures) requiring standards-based instruction in all content-area levels.	Standards-based instruction and assessment is systemic and systematic. Decision making regarding instructional resources is based on standards alignment. Existing resources and/or programs are aligned or abandoned.	Standards-based practices and processes are reviewed, edited, and revised at least twice on a regular cycle.	The organization's procedures and policies have served as benchmarks or templates for other organizations.

STANDARDS-BASED DESIGN — Instruction

Traits	Awareness	Understanding	First Implementation	Routine Use	Refinement	Replication
Instructional Model	The organization desires the development of a systemic, comprehensive instructional model (for example, students have increased access to applied learning activities, receive instruction at their developmental level, and progress is determined by performance-based demonstration of standards mastery).	The organization is developing a systemic, comprehensive instructional model. Staff development focuses on standards-based instructional techniques and strategies, allowing stakeholders to compare traditional and standards-based systems.	The organization has implemented a systemic, comprehensive instructional model. Staff development focuses on specific instructional strategies, aligns to current research, and provides opportunities for stakeholder feedback.	The organization's comprehensive instructional model is systemic and systematic. Continued implementation and staff development is provided by leaders from some stakeholder groups, aligns to stakeholder needs and current research. Plans are implemented for regular refinement.	The organization's comprehensive instructional model is reviewed, edited, and revised at least twice on a regular cycle. Staff development is driven by leaders from many stakeholder groups.	At the request of other organizations, the organization is able to provide staff development to assist in the creation and implementation of a comprehensive instructional model.
Student Focus	The organization desires to create individualized learning environments and experiences that lead to authentic student engagement (for example, students are placed at developmental content-area levels, participate in instructional design, and establish individual and classroom goals).	The organization creates professional development opportunities that provide strategies and tools for staff and students to individualize learning experiences and increase levels of engagement (for example, PLPs, student self-assessment, formal student feedback processes, and analytical assessment development).	The organization has integrated strategies and tools into the comprehensive instructional model allowing staff and students to individualize learning experiences and increase levels of engagement.	The organization's tools and strategies are systemic and systematic. Teachers and students value and benefit from individualized learning experiences and engagement levels show positive growth trends.	The organization's individualization and engagement tools and strategies are reviewed, edited, and revised at least twice on a regular cycle. Organization experiences sustained (3 years) positive growth trends.	The organization makes available and supports other organizations choosing to adopt its engagement strategies and tools.

STANDARDS-BASED DESIGN

Recording and Reporting

Traits	Awareness	Understanding	First Implementation	Routine Use	Refinement	Replication
Input	The organization is aware of the need to develop strategies for stakeholders to compare current and standards-based recording and reporting systems. The organization supports the gathering of stakeholder input on standard-based system features.	The organization begins providing stakeholders opportunities to compare current and standards-based recording and reporting system and the gathering of stakeholder input on standards-based system features.	The organization's recording and reporting system processes and products reflect stakeholder input.	Improvements to the system continue to reflect stakeholder input. Stakeholders begin to explain and defend the benefits of the recording and reporting process in a standards-based system.	Improvements to the system are driven by stakeholder input. The majority of stakeholders can explain and defend the benefits of the recording and reporting process in a standards-based system.	Stakeholders advocate for the adoption of standards-based recording and reporting systems at local, state, or national levels.
Development and Deployment	The organization is aware of the need to provide professional development to stakeholders on the use and implementation of an electronic recording and reporting system to monitor student progress on individual standards.	The organization initiates the training of stakeholders, providing tools and strategies to access and use student data, and is actively pursuing the adoption or creation of an electronic recording and reporting system.	The organization has begun implementation of an electronic recording and reporting system. Stakeholders begin use of the system and demonstrate increased understanding of the recording and reporting process in a standards-based system.	The organization's recording and reporting system use is systemic and systematic. Staff, students, and parents routinely access the system to monitor content-area-level progress. Staff and students use the system for planning class and individual student learning goals, and analysis of individual and organizational data.	The organization's recording and reporting system has been reviewed, edited, and revised at least twice on a regular cycle. The system has been modified to collect and report on data specific to focus-area progress.	The organization's recording and reporting system has been adopted by other organizations.

STANDARDS-BASED DESIGN — *Assessment*

Traits	Awareness	Understanding	First Implementation	Routine Use	Refinement	Replication
Development and Deployment	The organization is aware of the need to create standards-based internal assessments aligned to local standards and state assessment expectations and is willing to provide professional development on the use of standards-based assessment types (such as skills, analytical, self, and peer).	The organization has developed a plan to create and implement internal assessments with supporting procedures and policies to systematize student progress through all content-area levels. The organization is beginning to use standards-based assessments.	The organization has developed at least one assessment type for each content-area level. Systematized procedures and policies are in place to advance students. Principals, teachers, and students demonstrate understanding and use of the assessment processes and procedures.	The organization demonstrates systematic use of internal standards-based assessment types to assess mastery in all content-area levels. Assessment activities begin to involve parents. Data collection begins on inter-rater reliability. Plans and procedures are in place to review and refine assessments.	The organization's assessments are reviewed, edited, and revised at least twice on a regular cycle, and student performance indicates high degree of predictability for success on external assessments. Assessment activities involve parents and community members in formally assessing student performance.	Organizational assessment development and implementation processes serve as a benchmark for others.

SHARED VISION

Traits	Awareness	Understanding	First Implementation	Routine Use	Refinement	Replication
Input and Communication	The organization is aware of the need to identify essential stakeholder groups and has begun to communicate a need for shared vision focus areas.	All stakeholder groups are aware of formal processes for creating shared vision focus areas and had opportunities for input.	The organization has prioritized and communicated the input into focus areas; local standards reflect stakeholder input.	Representatives from every stakeholder group can articulate and defend the shared vision focus areas.	All stakeholder groups participate in and facilitate refinement of the shared vision focus areas; formal processes have been evaluated and refined at least twice on a regular cycle.	Processes have been established for each stakeholder group to help implement and assist other organizations in creating shared vision focus areas.

Traits	Awareness	Understanding	First Implementation	Routine Use	Refinement	Replication
Strategic Planning	The organization is aware of the need for shared vision focus areas, driven by a strategic plan, containing key performance indicators (KPIs) and supporting action plans.	The organization has begun to develop the strategic plan containing KPIs and supporting action plans aligned to the focus areas.	The organization begins implementation of a well-developed strategic plan aligned to the focus areas containing related KPIs and supporting action plans. The organization begins implementation of a well-developed strategic plan aligned to the focus areas containing related KPIs and supporting action plans.	The organization has fully implemented and evaluates the strategic plan progress based on KPIs. Evaluation is data driven and ensures alignment to the focus areas; appropriate adjustments are made to action plans.	The organization has an established cycle time to continuously refine the KPIs and related action plans aligned to the focus areas.	The organization assists other organizations in defining and refining action plans and goals tied to their focus areas.
Performance	The organization is aware of the need to formalize a process to analyze results and achievement tied to the focus areas (for example, dropout rate, cultural decline, school climate, test scores, teacher attrition rate, parent/ student involvement, curriculum relevance, and attendance).	The organization begins to identify and analyze data to measure progress on established KPIs and aligned focus areas.	The organization implements action plans and KPIs for the focus-area objectives. Staff begin to use the focus areas in the action planning process (for example, budget, curriculum, in-service schedule, committee work, school year schedule, and class schedule).	The entire organization uses the focus areas and associated KPIs in the action plan process (for example, budget, in-service schedule, business office, curriculum, school year schedule, and maintenance department). Performance on KPIs indicates progress on all focus-area objectives.	The organization applies a formal process to continuously review trend data on focus-area objectives and compares processes, tools, policies, and resource allocation with other organizations for analysis, modifications of action plans.	Formal processes for identification and analysis of KPIs are a benchmark for other organizations.

SHARED VISION

Traits	Awareness	Understanding	First Implementation	Routine Use	Refinement	Replication
Moral Purpose	The organization believes in making the best interests of students and hiring the right people based on its values and beliefs a top priority.	The organization is trustworthy and competent, has positive connections with stakeholders, and exemplifies strong, moral character.	The organization is courageous, confronts the brutal truth, and is willing to reinvent the organization for future opportunities.	The organization models and empowers others to use the lens of moral purpose in a systematic way to pursue organizational objectives.	The organization uses the lens of moral purpose to create a systemic evaluation process to review organizational objectives.	The organization sees no boundaries for helping other organizations prosper.
Relationships	The organization appreciates the benefits of open and candid dialogue amongst staff.	The organization promotes positive relations among its workers through tools and processes.	The organization has a systematic process to promote positive relationships among all stakeholders that positively impacts student learning and school culture.	The organization's positive relations and recognition of others' achievement allow new ideas and processes to be deployed that lead to breakthrough performances.	The organization demonstrates sustainability even with attrition of key leaders; collegiality and high organizational results continue.	Effective processes and tools are developed to assist other organizations in promoting positive relations.
Vision	The organization is aware of the need to communicate to all stakeholders the history and development of the current vision.	The organization leads and engages stakeholders in the (re)creation of a vision to positively impact student learning and school culture.	The organization designs, delivers, and communicates stakeholders' shared vision including systemic leadership development, performance-based systems, and continuous improvement.	The organization aligns resources, policies, and procedures to support stakeholders' shared vision, systemic leadership development, performance-based systems, and continuous improvement.	The organization sustains positive performance trends and improved cycle times for achievement in leadership development, performance-based systems, and stakeholders' shared vision.	Organizational procedures are available to assist other organizations in the creation and pursuit of their shared vision.

LEADERSHIP

Traits	Awareness	Understanding	First Implementation	Routine Use	Refinement	Replication
Change Adept	The organization recognizes its role and responsibility to create healthy working environments through clear expectations, collaboration, effective communication, and promotion of healthy relationships.	The organization accepts responsibility for results and researches new opportunities for becoming a high-performing system. The organization works to increase stakeholder understanding of change theory.	The organization embraces the change process and promotes from its values and beliefs new innovations that inspire lively discussions about high-performing systems.	The organization initiates new ideas that are goal oriented and systemic in nature. Leaders are willing to accept some dissent and ambiguity to improve the organization.	Organizational innovations lead to refinement of tools, policies, processes, and systematic deployment of ongoing improvement strategies to increase results. New paradigms are possible and encouraged.	Results from years of continued systemic improvement that have yielded clear processes are available for other organizations.
Results	The organization recognizes the need to analyze all current data to better understand existing performance levels.	The organization benchmarks internally and externally, analyzing the results to develop plans for continuous improvement.	The organization understands and applies processes for continuous improvement (for example, PDSA) using the shared vision focus areas as the driving force for improvement.	Internal and external organizational results indicate steady progress in the shared vision focus areas.	Internal and external organizational results indicate positive trends in all focus areas, yielding the greatest results in the organization.	Sustained positive results become a benchmark for other organizations. Internal and external results are world class.

LEADERSHIP

Traits	Awareness	Understanding	First Implementation	Routine Use	Refinement	Replication
Systemic and Systematic	The organization is aware that continuous improvement processes that are repeatable and provide opportunities for evaluation can lead to increased performance throughout the entire organization (for example, systematic use of PDSA in all organizational departments).	The organization understands the continuous improvement process, provides training, and recognizes the need to implement the process throughout all facets of the organization (for example, standards-based design, shared vision, and leadership).	The organization implements systemic continuous improvement strategies to increase performance in focus-area KPIs throughout the organization. Processes are becoming automatic or habitual.	The organization has fully implemented systemic continuous improvement strategies resulting in positive progress on focus-area KPIs throughout the organization. Stakeholders find process use efficient and advantageous.	The organization has fully implemented systemic continuous improvement strategies resulting in sustained (3 years) progress on focus-area KPIs throughout the organization.	Organizational and individual PDSAs serve as a benchmark for other organizations.
Evaluation Criteria	The organization is aware that there are several models that support the evaluation of systemic processes (such as Baldrige National Quality Program, Six Sigma, or ISO 9000 criteria).	The organization has given training to key stakeholders, increasing understanding of the basic model criteria (for example, information analysis and process management).	The organization has begun to use evaluation criteria in strategic planning and daily work.	The organization has implemented evaluation criteria to assess organizational processes.	The organization uses the evaluation criteria to revise and deploy plans to improve organizational processes.	The organization assists others in the revision and deployment of plans based on evaluation criteria.

CONTINUOUS IMPROVEMENT

Traits	Awareness	Understanding	First Implementation	Routine Use	Refinement	Replication
Cycle Times	The organization is aware of existing cycle times and that improving cycle times increases responsiveness to stakeholder and organizational needs.	The organization begins to compile cycle time data for organizational processes. Cycle times are compared to other successful organizations.	The organization establishes cycle times for key processes aligned to focus-area KPIs.	The organization's cycle times are established for all key processes and are being reduced; there are documented increases in organizational responsiveness and associated performances.	The organization's cycle times are regularly monitored and refined.	The organization has developed procedures that assist other organizations in improving efficiency and results.
Results	The organization is aware of the need to analyze results (such as revenue, facilities, education services, stakeholder satisfaction, and graduation follow-up) across the organization to better understand current performance.	The organization understands how to compile, benchmark, and communicate results that measure organizational performance.	The organization implements plans to document results aligned to focus-area KPIs, standards-based design, shared vision, and leadership.	The organization has documented positive trend lines in focus-area KPIs, standards-based design, shared vision, and leadership.	Refinements to the strategic plan result in documented 3-year positive trend lines.	Organizational results inspire others to invent new paradigms.

CONTINUOUS IMPROVEMENT

RISC Organizational Self-Assessment Tool Glossary

Analytical Assessment: Tools used to measure application of skills and knowledge by evaluating the parts of the whole. Often these tools are called scoring guides or rubrics.

Benchmark: Measurement according to specified standards in order to compare and improve one's own process or product.

Carnegie Unit: The number of hours a student spends in a given class. Carnegie units also are known as credits.

Change Adept: The skills and abilities to navigate and adapt to change for improvement.

Comprehensive Instructional Model: A formal instructional approach along a continuum of experiences from direct skills-based instruction to real-life application of skills and knowledge. This approach includes systematic tools, processes, and planning templates that assist staff with delivery and communication. The associated tools, processes, and templates are input driven, which allows for significant and consistent opportunities for student contributions in the design, delivery, and assessment phases of the Comprehensive Instructional Model.

Content-Area Levels: All content areas and levels that have been established from synthesized stakeholder input. Each area holds a continuum of standards that describe what students will need to know and be able to do to demonstrate mastery of a given content area. Each level is a developmental portion of the standards continuum for a given content area. Sample content areas are mathematics, science, technology, reading, writing, social sciences, service learning, career development, cultural development, and character development.

Continuous Improvement: Formal processes designed to appraise current practice and results to reveal improvements. These processes include systematic and systemic feedback, evaluation, and benchmarking cycles.

Cycle Time: The time required to fulfill commitments or to complete tasks. Time measurements play a major role because of the great importance of responsiveness. *Cycle time* refers to all aspects of time performance.

Cycle time improvement might include the time to respond to changing student and stakeholder needs, design time for new programs and processes, achievement time for students to meet content-area levels, or other key measures of time.

Deployment: The extent to which developed tools, plans, processes, and/or approaches are applied. Deployment is evaluated on the basis of the breadth and depth of application of the tools, plans, processes, and/or approaches to relevant work units within the organization. Deployment can occur in multiple stages (such as in year 1, standards in reading, writing, math, and character development are deployed; in year 2, all remaining content areas are deployed).

Development: Strategic designs of tools, plans, processes, and/or products. The designs often include input from stakeholders and use plan, do, study, act (PDSA) cycles to ensure measurement and refinement for maximum benefit of all stakeholders. For example, development cycles occur relative to local standards, internal assessments, and reporting tools.

Evaluation Criteria: An established set of standards and indicators by which organizations measure performance. Examples include the Baldrige National Quality Program, International Organization for Standardization (ISO 9000), and Six Sigma Criteria.

Focus Areas: The identification of three to seven areas determined from synthesized stakeholder input. These focus areas are succinct key elements that drive the shared vision of the organization. Focus areas are communicated and revisited according to established cycle times. Example areas include cultural development, basic skills, school-to-life transition, accountability, character education, and technology.

Input: Contributions to the education system. Examples of contributions include what students should know and be able to do, satisfaction with report card formats, and assessment of student performance on local standards. Input may be gathered through various strategies such as community and staff meetings, surveys, and interviews.

Instruction: The collection of strategies, processes, and tools used with students to facilitate learning. Instruction is aligned to standards and modified based on individual student needs, interests, and feedback. Instruction includes a continuum of experiences from direct skills-based instruction to real-life application of skills and knowledge.

Internal Assessments: Organizationwide measurement of student performance on standards in a variety of ways. Internal assessments are used to move students from one content-area level to the next on a developmental report card. A variety of internal assessments are used to provide multiple opportunities for students to demonstrate their knowledge and application of skills. These assessment types include skills-based, analytical, self, and peer assessments.

Key Performance Indicator (KPI): A quantifiable measurement, agreed to beforehand, that reflects the critical success factors of an organization. KPIs help an organization define and measure progress toward organizational goals. Once an organization has analyzed its mission, identified all of its stakeholders, and defined its goals, it needs a way to measure progress toward those goals. Key performance indicators are those measurements.

Leadership: The degree to which an organization has the capacity to utilize and develop the strengths and potential of each stakeholder to achieve superior performance relative to the shared vision.

Local Standards: Organizationwide student performance objectives for all content-area levels. Standards are developed based on stakeholder input collected during the shared vision process. They are aligned to or include state standards.

Moral Purpose: Making a positive difference in the lives of stakeholder groups and society as a whole by intense commitment to betterment, paying attention to process and product, treating others fairly, and being morally diligent in decision making.

Organization: A school, school district, nonprofit, or business, inclusive of all staff.

Performance: The manner in which an organization and/or its stakeholders achieve predetermined objectives or key performance indicators (KPIs). Example objectives include positive trends in focus areas, school-to-life transition, predictability of student success on state-level exams, state-level achievement results, and attendance.

Performance Task: Learning activities that are driven by standards and require application of knowledge and skills. They are assessed by specific criteria that mirror the task and the standards. The tasks may range from brief activities to long-term complex projects.

Personal Learning Plan: A student-driven goal-setting process (called plan, do, study, act, or PDSA) that is written and used by students, teachers, and parents. Goals are tied to local standards, internal assessments, and report cards.

Processes: Linked activities with the purpose of producing a program or service for students and/or stakeholders within or outside the organization. Generally, processes involve combinations of people, machines, tools, techniques, materials, and improvements in a defined series of steps or actions. Processes rarely operate in isolation and must be considered in relation to the processes that impact them. In some situations, processes might require adherence to a specific sequence of steps, with documentation (sometimes formal) of procedures and requirements, including well-defined measurements (such as administration of internal assessments and personal learning plans).

Recording and Reporting: The processes and tools used to document and communicate student progress on standards.

Relationships: Interactions between two or more people. Relationships are developed through positive and satisfying interactions.

Results: Outputs and outcomes achieved by the organization. Results are evaluated on the basis of current performance; performance relative to appropriate comparisons; the rate, breadth, and importance of performance improvements; and the relationship of results measures to key organizational performance requirements.

RISC Approach to Schooling: A research- and standards-based approach that implements local standards within developmental levels with aligned internal assessments and reporting tools. The RISC approach is driven by a shared vision, fostered through leadership development, and sustained by continuous improvement processes.

Shared Vision: A commonly held set of beliefs or goals generated by all stakeholder groups. Shared vision drives all aspects of organizational decision making, measurements, and improvements. A mission statement and focus areas are established from these shared beliefs and goals.

Stakeholder: A person or group within or outside a school system, which can impact or be affected by student success. Stakeholders may include but are not limited to the following people or organizations: students, tribal councils, families, teachers, classified staff, administrators, parents, community members, businesses, colleges, universities, and legislators.

Standards-Based Design: An education system in which students are placed in developmentally appropriate content-area levels and receive instruction along a continuum of experiences from direct skills-based instruction to real-life application of skills and knowledge. Progress is based upon students' demonstration of mastery on internal assessments (not on time or age); report cards reflect progress towards mastery of individual standards and content-area levels.

Strategic Planning: A systematic method used by an organization to anticipate and adapt to expected changes. Strategic plans are aligned to the mission statement, use focus areas as broad goals, identify key objectives and key performance indicators under the focus areas, and have well-developed associated action plans.

Student Focus: Approaches that individualize instruction and enhance student engagement in the learning process and environment. Example student outputs include class goals, personal learning plans, analytical assessments designs, instructor and classroom environment evaluations, and self-assessment scores.

Systemic: Affecting or involving an entire system. Systemic education improvement models include input mechanisms and delivery processes for students, classified and certified staff, parents, community members, businesses, and post-secondary institutions.

Tools: A mechanism that grants a mechanical or mental advantage in completing a task. Tool use in education improvement models enhances development, deployment, evaluation, and refinement of practices and processes. Deployment of tools is systematic and systemic where appropriate.

Transition Plan: Plans that address the transition from one system to another. Transition plans include the identification of which student groups will engage in the current system, with the remainder to engage in future system. These plans may include graduation requirements (time versus performance system), report card formats, transcript documents, and eligibility requirements.

Vision: The desired future state of the organization. The vision describes where the organization is headed, what it intends to be, or how it wishes to be perceived in the future.

References

Alaska State Troopers, Alaska Bureau of Alcohol and Drug Enforcement. (2007). *2007 Annual drug report.* Anchorage, AK: Author. Accessed at http://www. dps.state.ak.us/ast/ABADE/docs/2007%20Annual%20Drug%20Report.pdf on September 12, 2008.

Ambach v. Norwick, U.S. Supreme Court, 441 U.S. 68 (1979).

Benbow, N. (2005, June 29). *2003 Youth Risk Behavior Survey (YRBS) summary of results from a representative sample of students from selected Chicago public high schools.* Accessed at www.oism.cps.k12.il.us/pdf/2003YRBS.pdf on September 12, 2008.

Brown v. Board Of Education, U.S. Supreme Court, 347 U.S. 483 (1954).

Canfield, J., & Hansen, M. V. (1993). *Chicken soup for the soul: 101 Stories to open the heart and rekindle the spirit.* Deerfield Beach, CA: Health Communications, Inc.

Center on Education Policy. (2006). *From the capital to the classroom: Year 4 of the No Child Left Behind Act.* Washington, DC: Author. Accessed at http://www.cep-dc. org/index.cfm?fuseaction=document.showDocumentByID&DocumentID= 59&varuniqueuserid=75058610608 on September 12, 2008.

Center on Education Policy. (2008, August). *State high school exit exams: A move toward end-of-course exams.* Washington, DC: Author. Accessed at http:// www.cep-dc.org/index.cfm?fuseaction=Page.viewPage&pageId=493&parent ID=481 on September 12, 2008.

Centers for Disease Control. (2002, May 24). Fetal Alcohol Syndrome—Alaska, Arizona, Colorado, and New York, 1995–1997. *Morbidity and Mortality Weekly Report, 51*(20), 433–435. Accessed at http://www.cdc.gov/mmwr/preview/ mmwrhtml/mm5120a2.htm#tab2 on September 12, 2008.

Centers for Disease Control. (2004, May 21). Youth risk behaviors surveillance: United States, 2003. *Mortality and Morbidity Report, 53*(SS01), 1–96. Atlanta, GA: Author (specifically, Table 27). Accessed at http://www.cdc.gov/mmwr/ preview/mmwrhtml/ss5302a1.htm on September 12, 2008. See also State of Alaska; Health and Social Services. (n.d.). Substance Abuse Prevention. Accessed at http://hss.state.ak.us/dbh/prevention/programs/substanceabuse/ default.htm on September 12, 2008.

Chugach Alaska Corporation. (2006). *The people.* Accessed at http://www.chugach-ak.com/historypeople.html on September 12, 2008.

Coleman, J. S., Campbell, E. Q., Hobson, C. J., McPartland, J., Mood, A. M., Weinfield, F. D., & York, R. L. (1966). *Equality of educational opportunity.* Washington, DC: U.S. Government Printing Office.

Coladarci, T., Smith, L., & Whiteley, G. (2005, June). *The Re-inventing Schools Implementation Monitoring Survey, Alaska Benchmark/High School Graduation Qualifying Examination Data, and Relationships Between the Two.* Contact the Reinventing Schools Coalition (www.reinventingschools.org) for a complete copy of this evaluation report.

Collins, J. (2002). *Good to great: Why some companies make the leap . . . and others don't.* New York: HarperCollins.

Cross City Campaign for Urban School Reform. (2005). *A delicate balance: District policies and classroom practice.* Chicago: Author. Accessed at http://www.issuelab.org/research/delicate_balance_district_policies_and_classroom_practices on September 12, 2008.

Dewey, J. (1916). *Democracy and education: An introduction to the philosophy of education.* New York: Macmillan.

Fullan, M. (1993). *Change forces: Probing the forces of educational reform.* Levittown, PA: Falmer Press.

Fullan, M. (2001). *Leading in a culture of change.* San Francisco: Jossey-Bass.

Fullan, M. (2003). *The moral imperative of school leadership.* Thousand Oaks, CA: Corwin Press.

Fullan, M. (2005). *Leadership and sustainability: Systems thinkers in action.* Thousand Oaks, CA: Corwin Press

Gaddy, B. B., Hall, T. H., & Marzano, R. J. (1996). *School wars: Resolving our conflicts over religion and values.* San Francisco: Jossey-Bass.

Goldsmith, S., Angvik, J., Howe, L., Hill, A., & Leask, L. (2004, May). *Status of Alaska Natives 2004.* Anchorage, AK: Institute of Social and Economic Research, University of Alaska, Anchorage. Accessed at http://www.iser.uaa.alaska.edu/Home/ResearchAreas/statusaknatives.htm on September 12, 2008.

Good, T. L., & Brophy, J. E. (1986). School effects. In M. C. Wittrock (Ed.), *Handbook of research on teaching* (3rd ed., pp. 570–602). New York: Macmillan.

Hall, D. (2005, June). *Getting honest about grad rates: How states play the numbers and students lose.* Washington, DC: The Education Trust. Accessed at http://www2.edtrust.org/NR/rdonlyres/C5A6974D-6C04-4FB1-A9FC-05938CB0744D/0/GettingHonest.pdf on September 12, 2008.

Heifetz, R. (1994). *Leadership without easy answers.* Cambridge, MA: Harvard University Press.

Highland Tech High. (n.d.-a). Standards and Rubrics. See Reading and literature, Rubrics, Reading L.1. AK: Author. Accessed at http://www.highlandtech.org/academics/standards_and_rubrics/index.php on September 12, 2008.

Highland Tech High. (n.d.-b), Standards and Rubrics. See Standards, Social Environments, L.1, L.2, L.3, L.4, L.5, and L.6. Accessed at http://www.highlandtech.org/academics/standards_and_rubrics/index.php on September 12, 2008.

Information Insights, Inc. (2005, November). *Honoring our past: Shaping our future: Enhancing and sustaining Alaska's FASD Project.* Fairbanks, AK: Author. Prepared for Alaska Department of Health and Social Services, Division of Behavioral Health, Office of FAS. Accessed at http://www.hss.state.ak.us/fas/Resources/publications/FASDFinalReport.pdf on September 12, 2008.

Johnson, J. F. C. (1999). *Origin of the name.* Anchorage, AK: Chugach Alaska Corporation. Accessed at http://www.chugach-ak.com/historyorigin.html on September 12, 2008.

Kendall, J. S. (2003). Setting standards in early childhood education. *Educational Leadership, 60*(7), 63–68.

Kendall, J. S., & Marzano, R. J. (2004). *Content knowledge: A compendium of standards and benchmarks for K–12 education* (4th ed.). Aurora, CO: Mid-continent Research for Education and Learning. Accessed at www.mcrel.org/standards-benchmarks/ on September 12, 2008.

Kuhn, T. (1962). *The structure of scientific revolutions.* Chicago: University of Chicago Press.

Laird, J., Cataldi, E. F., KewalRamani, A., and Chapman, C. (2008). *Dropout and completion rates in the United States: 2006* (NCES 2008–053). Washington, DC: National Center for Education Statistics, Institute of Education Sciences, U.S. Department of Education. Accessed at http://nces.ed.gov/pubsearch/pubsinfo.asp?pubid=2008053 on September 12, 2008.

Lambert, L. (1998). *Building leadership capacity in schools.* Alexandria, VA: Association for Supervision and Curriculum Development.

Lambert, L. (2002). A framework for shared leadership. *Educational Leadership, 59*(8), 39–40.

Lezotte, L. W. (1997). *Learning for all.* Okemos, MI: Effective Schools Products, Ltd.

Martin, M. O., & Kelly, D. L. (Eds.). (1996). *Third International Mathematics and Science Study (TIMSS) technical report, volume I: Design and development.* Chestnut Hill, MA: Center for the Study of Testing, Evaluation, and Educational Policy, Boston College. (See, specifically, section 1.2, "The Conceptual Framework for TIMSS.") ERIC Document Reproduction Service No. ED 406418) Accessed at http://www.eric.ed.gov/ERICDocs/data/ericdocs2sql/content_storage_01/0000019b/80/16/76/a5.pdf on September 12, 2008.

Marzano, R. J. (2000). *A new era of school reform: Going where the research takes us.* Aurora, CO: Mid-continent Research for Education and Learning.

Marzano, R. J. (2003). *What works in schools: Translating research into action.* Alexandria, VA: Association for Supervision and Curriculum Development.

Marzano, R. J. (2006). *Classroom assessment & grading that work.* Alexandria, VA: Association for Supervision and Curriculum Development. See also, Marzano, R. J. (2000). *Transforming classroom grading.* Alexandria, VA: Association for Supervision and Curriculum Development.

Marzano, R. (2007). *Leadership for second-order change.* [Handout]. Serious Systemic Reform. Conference: RISC/Marzano & Associates. Arvada, Colorado.

Marzano, R. J., Gaddy, B. B., & D'Arcangelo, M. (2004). *Classroom management that works: Video series facilitator's guide.* Alexandria, VA: Association for Supervision and Curriculum Development.

Marzano, R. J., Gaddy, B. B., Foseid, M. P., Foseid, M. C., & Marzano, J. (2005). *A handbook for classroom management that works.* Alexandria, VA: Association for Supervision and Curriculum Development.

Marzano, R. J., & Kendall, J. S. (1996). *A comprehensive guide to designing standards-based districts, schools, and classrooms.* Alexandria, VA: Association for Supervision and Curriculum Development.

Marzano, R. J., & Kendall, J. S. (with Gaddy, B. B.). (1999). *Essential knowledge: The debate over what American students should know.* Aurora, CO: McREL Institute.

Marzano, R. J., Norford, J. S., Paynter, D. E., Pickering, D. J., & Gaddy, B. B. (2001). *A handbook for classroom instruction that works.* Alexandria, VA: Association for Supervision and Curriculum Development.

Marzano, R. J., Waters, T, & McNulty, B. A. (2005). *School leadership that works: From research to results.* Aurora, CO: Mid-continent Research for Education and Learning.

Marzano, R. J., Zaffron, S., Zraik, L., Robbins, S. L., & Yoon, L. (1995, winter). A new paradigm for educational change. *Education, 116*(2), 162–173. Alabama: Project Innovation. Accessed at http://www.landmarkeducation.com/landmark_forum_independent_research_marzano.jsp on September 12, 2008.

Merriam-Webster. (2008). *Merriam-Webster online dictionary.* www.merriam-webster.com/

Murray, W. H. (1951). *The Scottish Himalayan expedition.* London: Dent & Sons Ltd.

National Association for Gifted Children. (2005). *Twice-exceptional (gifted with special needs).* Accessed at http://www.nagc.org/index.aspx?id=973 on September 12, 2008.

National Center for Education Statistics. (n.d.). *Highlights from the Trends in International Mathematics and Science Study (TIMSS) 2003: Introduction.* Accessed at http://nces.ed.gov/pubs2005/timss03/index.asp on September 12, 2008.

National Center for Education Statistics. (2004, November). *Issue brief: Educational attainment of high school dropouts 8 years later.* Accessed at http://nces.ed.gov/pubs2005/2005026.pdf on September 12, 2008.

National Center for Education Statistics. (2007a, June). *Mapping 2005 state proficiency standards onto the NAEP scales: Research and development report* (NCES 2007–482). U.S. Department of Education, National Center for Education Statistics, Washington, DC: U.S. Government Printing Office. Accessed at http://nces.ed.gov/nationsreportcard/pdf/studies/2007482.pdf on September 12, 2008.

National Center for Education Statistics. (2007b, June 4). NAEP Research e-Center. Percentages of fourth- and eighth-grade students in reading and mathematics meeting state proficiency standards and performing at or above the NAEP *Proficient* level, by state: 2005. Washington, DC: Author. Accessed at http://nces.ed.gov/nationsreportcard/researchcenter/statemapping_t1.asp on September 12, 2008.

National Center on Education and the Economy. (1990). *America's choice: High skills or low wages! The report of the commission on the skills of the American workforce.* Rochester, NY: Author. Accessed at http://www.skillscommission.org/pdf/High_SkillsLow_Wages.pdf on September 12, 2008.

National Center on Education and the Economy. (2007). *Tough choices or tough times: The report of the new commission on the skills of the American workforce: Executive summary.* Washington, DC: Author. Accessed at http://www.skillscommission.org/executive.htm on September 12, 2008.

National Commission on Excellence in Education. (1983). *A nation at risk: The imperative for educational reform.* Washington, DC: U.S. Government Printing Office. Accessed at http://www.ed.gov/pubs/NatAtRisk/risk.html on September 12, 2008.

National Institute of Standards and Technology, Baldrige National Quality Program. (2001). *Chugach application summary.* Accessed at www.baldrige.nist. gov/PDF_files/Chugach_Application_Summary.pdf on September 12, 1008.

National Institute of Standards and Technology. (2002). Remarks by the 2001 Baldrige Award Recipients: Baldrige acceptance speech by Nathaniel Moore, Chugach School District Student. Gaithersburg, MD: Author. Accessed at ww.nist.gov/public_affairs/releases/wh_remarks.htm#Winners on September 12, 2008.

National Institute of Standards and Technology. (2004, November 24). Four organizations receive Presidential Quality Award. *NIST Tech Beat.* Accessed at www.nist.gov/public_affairs/techbeat/tb2004_1124.htm on September 12, 2008.

National Institute of Standards and Technology. (2006, April 5). State, local, and regional Quality Award information. Accessed at www.quality.nist.gov/State_Local.htm on September 12, 2008.

National Institute of Standards and Technology. (2007, June 5). Frequently asked questions about the Malcolm Baldrige National Quality Award. Accessed at www.nist.gov/public_affairs/factsheet/baldfaqs.htm on September 12, 2008.

Oettingen, G., Hönig, G., & Gollwitzer, P. M. (2000). Effective self-regulation of goal attainment. *International Journal of Education Research, 33*, 705–732. Accessed at http://www.psych.nyu.edu/oettingen/OETTINGEN2000ATTAINMENT.pdf on September 12, 2008.

Partnership for 21st Century Skills. (n.d.). *State standards for the 21st century.* Tucson, AZ: Author. Accessed at http://www.21stcenturyskills.org/documents/StateStandards.pdf on September 12, 2008.

Re-Inventing Schools Coalition. (2005, October). RISC vs. similar districts. Unpublished report.

Re-Inventing Schools Coalition. (2007). *Organizational self-assessment tool.* Wasilla, AK: Author.

Roberts, R. (2000). Leading without control: Moving beyond the 'Principal-Do-Right' model of educational leadership. In P. Senge, N. Cambron-McCabe, T. Lucas, B. Smith, J. Dutton, & A. Kleiner (Eds.), *Schools that learn: A fifth discipline fieldbook for educators, parents, and everyone who cares about education* (pp. 411–418). New York: Doubleday.

Schreiber, R., & Battino, W. (2002). *A guide to reinventing schools.* Anchorage, AK: Chugach School District.

Sellers, N. (2002, November). Interview with Dr. Larry Lezotte. *Audio Journal.* Accessed at http://ali.apple.com/ali_media/Users/1000059/files/others/ lezotte_transcript.pdf on September 12, 2008.

Senge, P., Kleiner, A., Roberts, C., Ross, R., Roth, G., & Smith, B. (1999). *The dance of change: The challenges of sustaining momentum in learning organizations.* New York: Doubleday.

Sergiovanni, T. J. (1994). *Building community in schools.* San Francisco: Jossey-Bass.

State of Alaska, Department of Education and Early Development. (2005, September 21). *Fetal Alcohol Spectrum Disorders: Why is it important for Alaska's educators to understand alcohol related disabilities?* Accessed at http://www.eed. state.ak.us/tls/fasd/ on September 12, 2008.

State of Alaska, Alaska Department of Labor and Workforce Development. (2006, July 1). *Workforce info. Population estimates. Vintage 2006 estimates. Table 1.19. Alaska population by age, race alone and male/female, Vintage 2006 estimates.* Accessed at http://www.labor.state.ak.us/research/pop/estimates/TA7R06x.xls on September 12, 2008.

State of Alaska, Health and Social Services. (n.d.). Substance abuse prevention. Accessed at http://hss.state.ak.us/dbh/prevention/programs/substanceabuse/ default.htm on September 12, 2008.

Stiggins, R. (2005, December). From formative assessment to assessment FOR learning: A path to success in standards-based schools. *Phi Delta Kappan, 87*(4), 324–328. Accessed at http://www.assessmentinst.com/forms/FromFormat_ k0512sti.pdf on September 12, 2008.

Stiggins, R. J, Arter, J., Chappuis, J., & Chappuis, S. (2005). *Classroom assessment for student learning: Doing it right–using it well.* Portland, OR: Assessment Training Institute.

Swanson, B. (2008, April 1). *Cities in crisis: A special analytic report on high school graduation.* Bethesda, MD: Editorial Projects in Education Research Center. Accessed at http://www.americaspromise.org/uploadedFiles/ AmericasPromiseAlliance/Dropout_Crisis/SWANSONCitiesInCrisis040108. pdf on September 12, 2008.

U.S. Census Bureau. (2000a). American fact finder. Alaska—place. GCT-PH1. Population, housing units, area, and density: 2000. Census 2000 Summary File 1. Accessed at http://factfinder.census.gov/servlet/GCTTable?_bm= y&-geo_id=04000US02&-_box_head_nbr=GCT-PH1&-ds_name= DEC_2000_SF1_U&-format=ST-7 on September 12, 2008.

U.S. Census Bureau. (2000b). American fact finder. United States—states; and Puerto Rico. GCT-PH1-R. Population, housing units, area, and density (geographies ranked by total population): 2000. Census 2000 Summary File 1. Accessed at http://factfinder.census.gov/servlet/GCTTable?_bm=y&-geo_id=01000US&-_box_head_nbr=GCT-PH1-R&-ds_name=DEC_2000_SF1_U&-format=US-9S on September 12, 2008.

U.S. Census Bureau. (2007). American fact finder. United States—states; and Puerto Rico. GCT-T1. Population estimates. 2007 Population estimates. Accessed at http://factfinder.census.gov/servlet/GCTTable?_bm=y&-geo_id=01000US&-_box_head_nbr=GCT-T1&-ds_name=PEP_2007_EST&-_lang=en&-redoLog=false&-format=US-9&-mt_name=PEP_2007_EST_GCTT1R_US9S&-_sse=on on September 12, 2008.

U.S. Department of Education. (2002, January 8). No Child Left Behind Act. Pub. L. 107–110—Jan. 8, 2002, 115 Stat. 1425. Accessed at http://www.ed.gov/policy/elsec/leg/esea02/index.html on September 12, 2008.

U.S. Department of Labor. (2006, August). *America's dynamic workforce.* Washington, DC: Author. Accessed at http://www.dol.gov/asp/media/reports/workforce2006/ADW2006_Full_Text.pdf on September 12, 2008.

U.S. Department of Labor, Bureau of Labor Statistics (2008, June 27). *Number of jobs held, labor market activity, and earnings growth among the youngest baby boomers: Results from a longitudinal study.* Washington, DC: Author. Accessed at http://www.bls.gov/news.release/pdf/nlsoy.pdf on September 12, 2008.

U.S. Department of Labor, The Secretary's Commission on Achieving Necessary Skills. (1991, June). *What work requires of schools: A SCANS report for America 2000.* Retrieved from http://wdr.doleta.gov/SCANS/whatwork/whatwork.pdf

United States Senate Committee on Indian Affairs. (2000, October 4). Testimony of Julie Kitka, President, Alaska Federation of Natives, Oversight Hearing on Alcohol and Law Enforcement in Alaska. Before the Senate Committee on Indian Affairs. Accessed at http://indian.senate.gov/2000hrgs/alea_1004/kitka.pdf on September 12, 2008.

Watzlawick, P. Weakland, J., & Fisch, R. (1974). *Change: Principles of problem formation and problem resolution.* New York: Norton and Company.

Whittle, C. (2005). *Crash course: Imagining a better future for public education.* New York: Riverhead Books, Penguin Group.

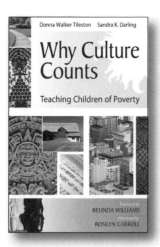

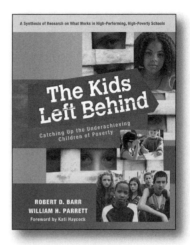

Why Culture Counts: Teaching Children of Poverty

Donna Walker Tileston and Sandra K. Darling
Foreword by Belinda Williams
Afterword by Rosilyn Carroll

Learn how to use students' cultural assets to close the achievement gap with these research-based methods of differentiating the context, content, and process of instruction. **BKF255**

Total Instructional Alignment: From Standards to Student Success

Lisa Carter

Replace an antiquated education system with a flexible, proactive one that ensures learning for all by focusing on three important domains of the alignment process. **BKF222**

The Kids Left Behind

Robert D. Barr and William H. Parrett

Successfully reach and teach the under-achieving children of poverty with the help of this comprehensive resource.

BKF216

Ahead of the Curve: The Power of Assessment to Transform Teaching and Learning

Edited by Douglas Reeves

Leaders in education contribute their perspectives of effective assessment design and implementation, sending out a call for redirecting assessment to improve student achievement and inform instruction.

BKF232

Solution Tree | Press

a division of
Solution Tree

Visit solution-tree.com or call 800.733.6786 to order.